The Constitution on Campus

The Constitution on Campus

A Guide to Liberty and Equality in Public Higher Education

William E. Thro
Charles J. Russo

ROWMAN & LITTLEFIELD
Lanham • Boulder • New York • London

Published by Rowman & Littlefield
An imprint of The Rowman & Littlefield Publishing Group, Inc.
4501 Forbes Boulevard, Suite 200, Lanham, Maryland 20706
www.rowman.com
86-90 Paul Street, London EC2A 4NE, United Kingdom

Copyright © 2022 by William E. Thro and Charles J. Russo

All rights reserved. No part of this book may be reproduced in any form or by any electronic or mechanical means, including information storage and retrieval systems, without written permission from the publisher, except by a reviewer who may quote passages in a review.

British Library Cataloguing in Publication Information Available

Library of Congress Cataloging-in-Publication Data Available

ISBN 978-1-4758-5680-4 (cloth) | ISBN 978-1-4758-5681-1 (pbk.)
  | ISBN 978-1-4758-5682-8 (ebook)

*To Julie,
my best friend, my wife, and the love of my life.
Thanks for growing old with me.
—Bill*

*To my wife, Debbie,
with all my undying love and affection,
now, always, and forever.
—Charlie*

Contents

Acknowledgments	ix
Introduction: No Angels on Campus: The Importance of the Constitution for Public Higher Education	xiii
Chapter 1: The Fixed Star: The Freedom of Speech	1
Chapter 2: The First Freedom: Religious Liberty on Campus	29
Chapter 3: Neither Knows nor Tolerates Classes: Equal Protection	47
Chapter 4: A Fundamental Value Determination: Procedural Due Process in Campus Disciplinary Proceedings	73
Chapter 5: The Double Security: Dual Sovereignty and State Constitutional Considerations	81
Chapter 6: The Will of the People, Not Their Agents: Judicial Enforcement of Federal Law and Immunity	97
Conclusion: But There Is Us: Public Higher Education and Hope for the Constitution	119
Appendix A: The Constitution of the United States	125
Appendix B: Additional Resources	149
About the Authors	159

Acknowledgments

WILLIAM E. THRO

This book is the latest stop on a journey that began when I first read the Constitution as an eleven-year-old Tenderfoot Boy Scout working on the Citizenship in the Nation merit badge. God has directed and guided my journey by allowing me to be blessed, privileged, honored, helped, inspired, assisted, and supported by some extraordinary people.

First, I was blessed to be born in the United States in the latter half of the twentieth century to parents who valued and encouraged education. Few people in human history have been so blessed with such opportunities, love, and support. God has given much, and much is expected.

Second, I was privileged to have outstanding mentors who advised me and guided me. Professor A.E. Dick Howard of the University of Virginia School of Law, Judge Ronald E. Meredith of the U.S. District Court for the Western District of Kentucky, Brian A. Snow, the first General Counsel of Colorado State University, and William H. Hurd, the first Solicitor General of Virginia, all taught me much about the Constitution and about life.

Third, I was fortunate to learn from some outstanding professors. George Curtis and Carl Metz at Hanover College, Jean Holmes at the University of Melbourne, Lillian Bevier, Peter Low, Bob O'Neil, and Bill Stuntz at the University of Virginia School of Law, emphasized the importance of a government of a sovereign People's Constitution, not of the People's Agents.

Fourth, I was honored to have the confidence and support of some outstanding leaders. Colorado Attorney General Gale Norton, Virginia Attorney General Jerry Kilgore, Virginia Attorney General Judy Jagdmann, Virginia Attorney General Bob McDonnell, Christopher Newport University President Paul Trible, and University of Kentucky President Eli Capilouto all took a chance by appointing me to positions of extraordinary responsibility requiring constant interaction with the Constitution.

Fifth, my scholarship has been helped by two exceptional co-authors. Professor Elizabeth Busch of Christopher Newport University collaborated with me on my first book, TITLE IX: THE TRANSFORMATION OF SEX DISCRIMINATION IN EDUCATION (2018) as well as other projects. Professor Charles Russo of the University of Dayton, my co-author on this work, has joined with me on numerous articles and book chapters. Both have shaped my thinking and writing.

Sixth, I have been inspired by numerous colleagues over the last three decades. Each of them has contributed in a significant way to how I think about the Constitution. While I could name literally dozens of people, I am particularly indebted to Scott Bauries, Ben Beaton, Bryan Beauman, Wes Butler, Steve Clifton, Paul Farley, Cliff Iler, Matt Kuhn, Peter Lake, Craig Lindwarm, Maureen Matsen, Steve McCullough, Chad Meredith, Bill Mims, Jim Newberry, Laurence Pendleton, Margaret Pisacano, Travis Powell, John Robinson, Paul Salamanca, Josh Salsburey, Shannan Stamper, Ashley Taylor, Farnaz Thompson, Tim Tymkovich, Jon White, Judge Wilson, Craig Wood, and George Wright.

Finally, and most importantly, my wife, Julie, and my son, Noah, have provided essential support. Without them, this book would not be possible.

CHARLES J. RUSSO

As with any book, many people deserve to be thanked, but four sets of people were extremely helpful in helping bring this book to fruition.

First, I would like to thank my Deans, Ali Carr-Chellman in the School of Education and Andrew Strauss in the School of Law along with my Chair in the Department of Educational Administration, David A. Dolph, for their friendship and support. I would also like to thank our President, Eric Spina, and Provost Paul Benson for the supportive environment they have worked to create on our campus.

Second, I would like to thank those who read this book and reflect on the importance of law in the day-to-day operations of public institutions of higher education.

Third, I would like to extend my special thanks to three of my former professors, all of whom are long-term personal and professional friends from my student days at St. John's University. Many thanks to the late Dr. David B. Evans, who, even while I was an undergraduate student of theology, taught me a great deal about the skills necessary to pursue an academic career. I would next like to thank the late Professor David L. Gregory from the School of Law for his support and friendship over the years. Finally, I express my deep appreciation to and fondness for my doctoral mentor, and close friend, Dr. Zarif F. Bacilious, Dean Emeritus of the School of Education and Human Services, for helping me to complete my studies and enter academe as he continues to offer me his sage counsel.

Fourth, and certainly not least, keeping in mind the often-cited maxim of Supreme Court Justice Joseph Story, that the law "is a jealous mistress and requires a long and constant courtship," I would like to express my undying love and devotion to my wife Debbie, to whom I dedicate this book, our daughter Emily, her husband Adriel, and our granddaughters Lorelai and Adelaide, plus our son David, his wife Li Hong, and our grandson, James Robert. I would also like to take this opportunity to thank Debbie most especially for her loving and generous assistance in helping with many facets of the book and our life together. I am truly blessed to have such a wonderful, loving family.

JOINT ACKNOWLEDGMENTS

First, we jointly offer our heartfelt thanks to our editors, Vice President for Acquisitions at Rowman & Littlefield, Dr. Tom Koerner, and Managing Editor Carlie Wall for their always gracious assistance and help in shepherding the proposal through to publication along with the many ways in which they offered their gracious assistance throughout the publication process. We also express our thanks to our copy editor.

Second, we would like to thank Jaren Hardesty, class of 2022 at the University of Dayton for School of Law for his fine efforts in cite checking, copyediting, and helping to prepare the final manuscript for final publication.

Third, we express our gratitude to Linda Speakman, Executive Assistant to the General Counsel of the University of Kentucky, for her editorial assistance in preparing the manuscript.

Introduction

No Angels on Campus: The Importance of the Constitution for Public Higher Education

> If men were angels, no government would be necessary. If angels were to govern men, neither external nor internal controls on government would be necessary. In framing a government which is to be administered by men over men, the great difficulty lies in this: you must first enable the government to control the governed; and in the next place oblige it to control itself.—James Madison[1]

The Constitution's Framing Generation, reflecting the dominant Calvinist theology[2] of late Eighteenth Century America,[3] assumed "there is never a moment in human history when that which is human can be trusted blindly as a force for good."[4] Not surprisingly, the United States Constitution embodies an "obsessive distrust of government—*all* government—and [the] elevation of law into the ruling power of the state. Indeed, the idea of law itself as *sovereign* is the key."[5] Because a republic "derives all its powers directly or indirectly from the great body of the people,"[6] sovereignty—the final, supreme, indivisible lawmaking authority—belongs to the People themselves.[7]

Establishing a Nation "conceived in liberty and dedicated to the proposition that all . . . created equal,"[8] the People, in the exercise of our sovereignty, established the Constitution "as a fixed fundamental law superior to ordinary [legislative or executive actions]."[9] By adopting the Constitution, the People both established and limited the government.[10] The words of the Constitution reflect the Will of the People, but the actions of government reflect the Will of the People's Agents, the legislators and executive officials who govern.[11] Because "the power of the people is superior to" the government, "where the will of the [government], declared in its statutes [and executive actions], stands in opposition to that of the people, declared in the Constitution," the fundamental law prevails.[12]

"To be sure, a constitution is a document that protects against future democratic excesses. But when it is adopted, it is adopted by democratic process. That is what legitimatizes it . . ."[13] Thus, "before the Constitution could take effect, the founders called on the states to convene special conventions of the people's representatives. And they insisted on a supermajority of those conventions to ratify the original Constitution."[14] The outcome of this effort was far from certain with New York rejecting and then ratifying the charter while two States, North Carolina, and Rhode Island, ratified the Constitution only after it became operational.[15]

Unlike the United Kingdom, where the "Crown in Parliament" can "make or unmake any law whatsoever" and no court can "override or set aside" a parliamentary act,[16] the People of the United States "deliberately rejected that model when they decided to adopt a written Constitution."[17] Recognizing England's failure to limit the monarch "brought civil war, a king's execution, the Cromwellian regime, restoration, and a bloodless revolution"[18] during the seventeenth century and reflecting the enduring influence of the 1215 Magna Carta,[19] We the People devised an "untouchable, fundamental law, to be interpreted not by Congress, still less by the President, but by Justices of the Supreme Court."[20]

By refusing to trust their leaders and embracing the idea of the Constitution as the fundamental law superior to ordinary governmental actions, the sovereign People established a Government of the Constitution, not of the People's Agents.[21] Such an arrangement reflects "a principle of distrust of every person who holds power—Christian or not—combined with a hope that a well-designed system could deter the inevitable temptations to abuse power."[22] To secure the "self-evident truths" of the Declaration,[23] We the People imposed limitations on government, empowered the judiciary to enforce those limitations, and suggested courts must be confined to principled interpretations and constructions of the Constitution. Each of these three aspects warrants further elaboration.

First, the Constitution imposes internal and external limits on governmental power. There are "certain specified exceptions to the legislative [and executive] authority"[24] which withdraws "certain subjects from the vicissitudes of political controversy" and "places them beyond the reach of majorities and officials."[25] Recognizing the dangers of concentrating power, the Constitution "protects us from our own best intentions" by preventing the concentration of "power in one location as an expedient solution to the crisis of the day."[26] Instead of an all-powerful national government,[27] the Constitution "split the atom of sovereignty . . . establishing two orders of government [federal and state], each with its own direct relationship, its own privity, its own set of mutual rights and obligations to the people who sustain it and are governed by it."[28]

Regardless of whether the source of the limitation is from the division of sovereignty, the constitutional structure, or the constitutional text, the Constitution imposes both requirements and prohibitions on constitutional actors.[29] In the space between what the Constitution requires and what the Constitution prohibits, elected legislative and executive actors have absolute discretion to pursue whatever policy objectives they desire. Moreover, within this constitutional space, the legislative and executive actors can choose how to remedy the constitutional violation.[30]

Second, because our constitutional actors are imperfect humans, there will be times, "where the will of the legislature, declared in its statutes, stands in opposition to that of the people, declared in the Constitution. . . . "[31] "Whenever a particular statute [or executive action] contravenes the Constitution, it will be the duty of judicial tribunals to adhere" to the Constitution and declare the statutes and executive actions void.[32] Therefore, the judiciary "will not shrink from our duty 'as the bulwar[k] of a limited constitution against legislative encroachments.'"[33] If, as Alexis de Tocqueville suggested, every political question becomes a judicial one, then judicial review of the actions of other constitutional actors will be the norm.[34]

The Supreme Court must enforce all constitutional provisions. Because "words cannot be meaningless, else they would not have been used,"[35] every constitutional provision limits the discretion of some constitutional actor in some way.[36] While there may be circumstances where constitutional actors are entitled to great deference, such as the conduct of military operations in wartime, "[i]t is no more the court's function to revise by subtraction than by addition. A provision that seems to the court unjust or unfortunate . . . must nonetheless be given effect."[37]

This power of judicial enforcement goes beyond simply declaring a constitutional actor in violation of the Constitution. In *Cooper v. Aaron*,[38] the Supreme Court of the United States declared its "interpretation of [the Constitution] is the supreme law of the land"[39] even though the other branches or the States may interpret the Constitution differently.[40] After *Cooper*, constitutional actors must "follow the Court's interpretations, not just in the particular case announcing those interpretations, but in similar cases as well."[41] In America, "the government can and does lose in its own courts and then respect those judgements."[42]

Third, because judges are not perfect, but flawed humans, there must be meaningful limits on how the judiciary interprets the Constitution. The Court has "a vital responsibility to enforce the rule of [the Constitution], which is critical to a free society."[43] Yet, because its constitutional decisions are binding on the other Branches of the National Government and the States, courts are tempted to become "a bevy of Platonic Guardians,"[44] who "substitutes their predictive judgments for those of elected legislatures and expert agencies."[45] Conversely, judges should avoid the temptation to ignore the Constitution and simply defer to the judgment of legislators, bureaucrats, or university administrators.[46]

To preserve "the rule of [the Constitution] from the dictatorship of a shifting Supreme Court majority, . . . judicial opinions should be grounded in consistently applied principle."[47] When the Constitution is "interpreted, as it ought to be interpreted," then "the Constitution is a glorious liberty document."[48] Courts should reject "the conviction that the Constitution's meaning *changes* over time and that *judges* should determine what changes should be made based on external policy considerations."[49] Despite the appeal of constitutional theories advocating the "common good" or "democracy,"[50] the judiciary should not "exercise *Will* instead of *Judgment*" or the "substitution of their pleasure to that of" the People's elected officials.[51]

Rather, the judiciary must accept "the Constitution's meaning was fixed at its ratification [or the ratification of the amendment] and the judge's job is to discern and apply that meaning to the people's cases and controversies."[52] As Constitutions were "written to be understood by the voters, its words and phrases were used in their normal and ordinary meaning as distinguished from technical meaning,"[53] the judiciary may embrace "an idiomatic meaning," but it must reject "secret or technical meanings that would not have been known to ordinary citizens" at the time the Constitution was adopted.[54] Indeed, a Government of the People's Constitution rather than the People's Agents requires jurists to focus on the meaning of the words of the law, not the desires of those who passed or interpret the provision.[55]

As the Supreme Court observed: "If judges could add to, remodel, update, or detract from old statutory terms . . ., we would risk amending statutes outside the legislative process . . . [a]nd we would deny the people the right to continue relying on the original meaning of the law."[56] Ultimately, "the limits of the drafters' imagination supply no reason to ignore the law's demands. When the express terms of a statute give us one answer and extratextual considerations suggest another, it's no contest. Only the written word is the law, and all persons are entitled to its benefit."[57]

In short, "We the People," not the monarch, parliament, or the government in general, have sovereignty—the final, supreme, indivisible lawmaking authority. In the exercise of our sovereignty, the People established the Constitution "as a fixed fundamental law superior to ordinary legislation"[58] and, thus, created and limited the government.[59] The idea of a sovereign People establishing a fundamental law creating and limiting the government has three profound implications for higher education.

First, a state college or university, through its administrators, and, in some contexts, its faculty and students, are constitutional actors.[60] This statement surprises many who work in public higher education. Because students, staff, faculty members, and visitors do not "shed their constitutional rights . . . at the [university] gate," those who act on behalf of public colleges and universities are constitutional actors, the paramount duty is to obey the Constitution.[61] The constitutional obligations trump other duties under statutes, regulations, guidance documents, union agreements, internal policies, or faculty rules.[62]

Second, because "there is a degree of depravity in mankind which requires a certain degree of circumspection and distrust," university administrators are no more virtuous than other governmental actors.[63] Like other government officials, higher education administrators may pursue their own interests at the expense of the public interests, may reward their friends and punish their enemies, and may subordinate the constitutional rights of others to their own well-intentioned policy objectives. Constitutional conflict and constitutional litigation are inevitable. Like government officials outside of academe, a public college or university's constitutional actors must ensure their own behavior conforms to the Constitution while striving to ensure their colleagues also comply.

Third, a sizable portion of constitutional law involves public education, whether at the K–12 or postsecondary level. Outside of public education, most Americans do not encounter government except to pay their taxes, obtain and renew their licenses, and the occasional speeding ticket. Even so, most parents send their children to public schools and most college students attend public institutions. Thus, if the average person is going to have a dispute with the government over their constitutional rights, such conflicts likely are going to involve public education. Indeed, many of the Supreme Court's landmark decisions on freedom of speech,[64] religious liberty,[65] race,[66] sex,[67] due process,[68] state constitutional considerations,[69] and immunity[70] involve public higher education.

Our purpose in authoring this book is to provide a user-friendly guide to constitutional law in the context of public colleges and universities that is easily accessible to students, faculty members, and administrators. While we hope this book is helpful to lawyers, our primary audience is the educated layperson. There are extensive end notes with citations to cases and scholarly books and articles, but, unlike law reviews, none of these citations are substantive. Instead, we have kept our discussions of substantive issues in the text. This means readers are free to ignore the citations if they wish unless they are looking for additional background and/or resources.

Each of the book's chapters discusses the basic constitutional principles and how they apply in the context of public higher education. More specifically, this volume covers Freedom of Speech, Religious Liberty, Equal Protection,

Due Process, Dual Sovereignty and State Constitutional Considerations, and Immunity and Injunctive Relief. At the end of each chapter, there is a summary of the major cases discussed in the chapter. In addition, there are two appendixes—one consisting of the entire text of the United States Constitution and another with suggestions for further reading.

While the requirements and prohibitions of the Fourth, Fifth, Sixth, Seventh, and Eighth Amendments do apply to public colleges and universities, particularly their institutional police departments, we omit discussions of criminal procedure. This is consistent with the typical practice in constitutional law texts and guides.

Similarly, although officials at public colleges and universities are constrained by a variety of federal laws including Title VII,[71] Title IX,[72] Section 504,[73] and the Americans with Disabilities Act,[74] the scope of this book is limited to the Constitution and does not include a comprehensive discussion of those statutes.

Finally, while this book discusses the application of constitutional law to a variety of different situations in the context of public campuses, **it is not intended to be legal advice**. As such, because it is important for readers to keep in mind that the differences between constitutional and unconstitutional actions often turn on the most subtle of facts. This book is a start, not the finish. Thus, when disputes arise, individuals should consult their own legal counsel in determining how to proceed.

NOTES

1. THE FEDERALIST NO. 51 (James Madison).
2. James H. Smylie, *Madison and Witherspoon: Theological Roots of American Political Thought*, 73 AMERICAN PRESBYTERIANS 155 (1995).
3. Mark David Hall, ROGER SHERMAN AND THE CREATION OF THE AMERICAN REPUBLIC 12–40 (2013).
4. Marci Hamilton, *The Calvinist Paradox of Distrust and Hope at the Constitutional Convention*, in CHRISTIAN PERSPECTIVES ON LEGAL THOUGHT 293, 295 (Michael W. McConnell, Robert F. Corchran, Jr., & Angela C. Carmella, eds., 2001).
5. David Starkey, MAGNA CARTA: THE MEDIEVAL ROOTS OF MODERN POLITICS 1308 (2015) (Kindle Edition) (emphasis original).
6. THE FEDERALIST NO. 39 (James Madison).
7. Gordon S. Wood, CONSTITUTIONALISM IN THE AMERICAN REVOLUTION 18–26, 92–95 (2021).
8. Abraham Lincoln, GETTYSBURG ADDRESS (1863).
9. Wood, *supra* note 7, at 48.
10. *Id.* at 47–52, 92–95.
11. THE FEDERALIST NO. 78 (Alexander Hamilton).

12. *Id.*

13. *Nomination of Judge Antonin Scalia to be Associate Justice of the Supreme Court of the United States*, 99th Cong. 89 (1986) (statement of Antonin Scalia).

14. Neil Gorsuch, A REPUBLIC, IF YOU CAN KEEP IT 119 (2019).

15. Pauline Maier, RATIFICATION: THE PEOPLE DEBATE THE CONSTITUTION (2010).

16. Martin Loughlin, THE BRITISH CONSTITUTION: A VERY SHORT INTRODUCTION 32 (2013).

17. Gorsuch, *supra* note 14, at 116.

18. A.E. Dick Howard, THE ROAD FROM RUNNYMEDE: MAGNA CARTA AND CONSTITUTIONALISM IN AMERICA 9 (1968) (paperback edition 2015).

19. *Id.* 14–98 (discussing the influence of Magna Carta in the Colonial Charters, the New England Covenants, the Proprietary Colonies, and Pennsylvania).

20. Starkey, *supra* note 5, at 1312.

21. THE FEDERALIST No. 78 (Alexander Hamilton).

22. Marci A. Hamilton, *The Framers, Faith, and Tyranny*, 26 ROGER WILLIAMS U. L. REV. 495, 500 (2021).

23. DECLARATION OF INDEPENDENCE ¶ 2.

24. THE FEDERALIST No. 78 (Alexander Hamilton).

25. *West Virginia State Board of Education v. Barnette*, 319 U.S. 624, 638 (1943).

26. *New York v. United States*, 505 U.S. 144, 187 (1992).

27. *McCulloch v. Maryland*, 17 U.S. (4 Wheat.) 316, 405 (1819).

28. *U.S. Term Limits v. Thornton*, 514 U.S. 779, 838 (1995) (Kennedy, J. concurring).

29. William E. Thro, *No Clash of Constitutional Values: Respecting Freedom & Equality in Public University Sexual Assault Cases*, 28 REGENT UNIV. L. REV. 197 (2016).

30. *See Milliken v. Bradley*, 433 U.S. 267, 280–81(1977).

31. THE FEDERALIST NO. 78 (Alexander Hamilton).

32. *Id.*

33. *Northwest Austin Municipal Utility District No. One v. Holder*, 557 U.S. 193, 205 (2009).

34. Alexis de Tocqueville, DEMOCRACY IN AMERICA 310 (Arthur Goldhammer, trans., The Library of America ed. 2004) (1835).

35. *United States v. Butler*, 297 U.S. 1, 65 (1936).

36. Antonin Scalia & Bryan A. Garner, READING LAW: THE INTERPRETATION OF LEGAL TEXTS § 27 (2012).

37. *Id.*

38. *Cooper v. Aaron*, 358 U.S. 1 (1958).

39. *Id.* at 18–19.

40. Josh Blackman, *The Irrepressible Myths of Cooper v. Aaron*, 107 Geo. L.J. 1135, 1137 (2019).

41. Stephen Breyer, MAKING OUR DEMOCRACY WORK: A JUDGE'S VIEW 60 (2010).

42. Gorsuch, *supra* note 14, at 237.

43. Amy Coney Barrett, *Opening Statement*, CONFIRMATION HEARING OF JUDGE BARRETT TO BE ASSOCIATE JUSTICE OF THE SUPREME COURT OF THE UNITED STATES (October 12, 2020).

44. *Griswold v. Connecticut*, 381 U.S. 479, 526 (1965) (Black, J., dissenting) (quoting Learned Hand, THE BILL OF RIGHTS 70 (1958)).

45. *Lingle v. Chevron*, 544 U.S. 528, 544 (2005).

46. Charles J. Russo, *The Courts and Education Law: What Role Should Judges Play?* 13 INTERNATIONAL JOURNAL OF EDUCATION LAW AND POLICY 7 (2017).

47. *McCreary County v. ACLU*, 545 U.S. 844, 890–91 (2005) (Scalia, J., dissenting).

48. Frederick Douglass, WHAT TO THE SLAVE IS THE FOURTH OF JULY (1852)

49. Gorsuch, *supra* note 14, at 110.

50. *See, e.g.,* Adrian Vermeule, COMMON GOOD CONSTITUTIONALISM (2022); Stephen Breyer, ACTIVE LIBERTY (2005); Ronald Dworkin, LAW'S EMPIRE (1986); John Hart Ely, DEMOCRACY & DISTRUST (1979).

51. THE FEDERALIST No. 78 (Alexander Hamilton) (emphasis original).

52. Gorsuch, *supra* note 14, at 116.

53. *United States v. Sprague,* 282 U.S. 716, 731 (1931). *See also Gibbons v. Ogden,* 22 U.S. (9 Wheat.) 1, 188 (1824).

54. *District of Columbia v. Heller,* 554 U.S. 570, 576–77 (2008).

55. Antonin Scalia, A MATTER OF INTERPRETATION: FEDERAL COURTS AND THE LAW, 17 (Amy Gutmann ed., 1997).

56. *Bostock v. Clayton County* 140 S. Ct. 1731, 1737 (2020).

57. *Id.*

58. Wood, *supra* note 7, at 48.

59. *Id.* at 47–52, 92–95.

60. *Ward v. Polite,* 667 F.3d 727, 732–33 (6th Cir. 2012).

61. *Tinker v. Des Moines Indep. Cmty. School District,* 393 U.S. 503, 506, (1969).

62. *Marbury v. Madison,* 5 U.S. (1 Cranch) 137, 178 (1803).

63. THE FEDERALIST No. 55 (James Madison).

64. *Christian Legal Society v. Martinez,* 561 U.S. 661 (2010); *Board of Regents of University of Wisconsin System v. Southworth,* 529 U.S. 217 (2000); *Rosenberger v. Rector and Visitors of University of Virginia,* 515 U.S. 819 (1995); *Widmar v. Vincent,* 454 U.S. 263 (1981); *Healy v. James,* 408 U.S. 169 (1972); *Keyishian v. Board of Regents of University of State of New York,* 385 U.S. 589, (1967); *Sweezy v. New Hampshire,* 354 U.S. 234, (1957).

65. *Locke v. Davey,* 540 U.S. 712 (2004); *Rosenberger v. Rector and Visitors of University of Virginia,* 515 U.S. 819 (1995); *Widmar v. Vincent,* 454 U.S. 263 (1981).

66. *Fisher v. University of Texas,* 136 S. Ct. 2198 (2016) (*Fisher II*); *Fisher v. University of Texas,* 570 U.S. 297 (2013) (*Fisher I*). *Grutter v. Bollinger,* 539 U.S. 306 (2003); *Gratz v. Bollinger,* 539 U.S. 244 (2003); *Regents of the University of California v. Bakke,* 438 U.S. 265 (1978).

67. *United States v. Virginia,* 518 U.S. 515 (1996); *Mississippi University for Women v. Hogan,* 458 U.S. 718 (1982).

68. *Regents of the University of Michigan v. Ewing,* 474 U.S. 214 (1985); *Board of Regents of State Colleges v. Roth,* 408 U.S. 564 (1972).

69. *Schutte v. Coalition to Defend Affirmative Action, Integration, & Immigrant Rights & Fight for Equality by Any Means Necessary*, 572 U.S 291 (2014).

70. *Central Virginia Community College v. Katz*, 546 U.S. 356 (2006); *Tennessee Student Assistance. Corp. v. Hood*, 541 U.S. 440 (2004); *Lapides v. Board of Regents of the University Sys. of Georgia*, 535 U.S. 613, 617 (2002); *Board of Trustees of University of Alabama v. Garrett*, 531 U.S. 356 (2001); *Kimel v. Florida Board of Regents*, 528 U.S. 62 (2000); *College Savings Bank v. Florida Prepaid Postsecondary Educational Expense Board*, 527 U.S. 666 (1999); *Florida Prepaid Postsecondary Educational Expense Board v. College Savings Bank*, 527 U.S. 627 (1999); *Doe v. Regents of the University of California*, 519 U.S. 425 (1997).

71. 42 U.S.C. § 2000e et seq.

72. 20 U.S.C. § 1681 et seq.

73. 29 U.S.C. § 701 et seq.

74. 42 U.S.C. § 12101 et seq.

Chapter 1

The Fixed Star
The Freedom of Speech

> If there is any fixed star in our constitutional constellation, it is that no official, high, or petty, can prescribe what shall be orthodox in politics, nationalism, religion, or other matters of opinion or force citizens to confess by word or act their faith therein.—*West Virginia State Board of Education v. Barnette*[1]

The need for freedom of expression "in the community of American universities is almost self-evident."[2] "Universities have historically been fierce guardians of intellectual debate and free speech, providing an environment where students can voice ideas and opinions without fear of repercussion."[3] In describing his vision for the University of Virginia, Jefferson said, "we are not afraid to follow truth wherever it may lead, nor to tolerate any error so long as reason is left free to combat it."[4] Simply put, "knowledge cannot be advanced unless existing claims to knowledge can with freedom be criticized and analyzed."[5]

Disputes over "the truth" are resolved by facts, not feelings;[6] by science, not superstition; by debate, not dogma;[7] by discussion, not denunciation; by heterodoxy, not orthodoxy.[8] The purpose of higher education "is to be a place of facilitating disagreement across differences . . . 'place of constrained disagreement, of imposed participation in conflict.'"[9]

Ensuring "free speech is bred into the bones of a modern university,"[10] requires a campus culture committed to free expression.[11] Officials at every public institution have "a solemn responsibility not only to promote a lively and fearless freedom of debate and deliberation, but also to protect that freedom when others attempt to restrict it."[12] Rather, public campus officials must recognize the First Amendment withdraws protected speech "from the vicissitudes of political controversy" and places it "beyond the reach of majorities and officials."[13]

This six-part chapter details how the Freedom of Speech limits officials at public colleges and universities. Part I outlines General Principles of the Free Speech Clause. Part II explores how those principles apply to both individual students and student organizations on public college and university campuses. Part III discusses the rights of those who are employed by public institutions. Part IV examines academic freedom in both its constitutional and professional definitions. Part V discusses a possible exception to the general constitutional rules when faculty members engage in teaching or research. Specifically, whether this expression is considered speech in the faculty members' governmental capacities and, if so, subject to constitutional protection. Part VI summarizes the major cases discussed in this chapter.

I. GENERAL PRINCIPLES OF THE FREEDOM OF SPEECH

Freedom of Speech means "the government may not punish or suppress speech based on disapproval of the ideas or perspectives the speech conveys."[14] "The First Amendment itself reflects a judgment by the American people that the benefits of its restrictions on the Government outweigh the costs. Our Constitution forecloses any attempt to revise that judgment simply on the basis that some speech is not worth it."[15]

These statements surprise many in the public college and university community. There is a general belief that the scope of the Freedom of Speech is far narrower in scope than the Supreme Court has said. This part discusses the lack of a hate speech exception, the categorical exceptions to the Freedom of Speech, and the inability of the campus officials to compel speech.

A. No Hate Speech Exception

Because some expression may cause emotional harm for both individuals and groups, many public institution administrators believe such expression undermines the creation of a diverse and inclusive environment. This becomes evident when students and faculty frequently demand the institution punish "hate speech," which they loosely define as any expression they regard as racist, sexist, anti-LGBTQIA+, and religious bigotry. Although many members of public campus communities may believe there is "hate speech" exception to the Freedom of Speech, the Supreme Court has repeatedly held there is no hate speech exception. Three recent cases illustrate the point.

First, in *Snyder v. Phelps*,[16] the Supreme Court ruled a State could not impose civil liability for intentional infliction of emotional distress resulting from provocative and inflammatory comments made at the funeral of a United States Marine who was killed in the line of duty.[17] Despite the incendiary nature of the comments and the sensitive context, the Court decided the speech addressed the "the political and moral conduct of the United States and its citizens, the fate of our Nation, homosexuality in the military, and scandals involving the Catholic clergy,"[18] and thus, touched on a matter of public concern.[19] Because the speech was on a matter of public concern, the Court found it received "special protection" and "cannot be restricted simply because it is upsetting or arouses contempt."[20]

Second, in *Matal v. Tam*,[21] the Supreme Court unanimously concluded Congress violated the Constitution when it enacted a statute prohibiting the registration of trademarks that may "disparage . . . or bring . . . into contempt or disrepute" any "persons, living or dead."[22] In a dispute involving the Patent and Trademark Office's refusal to register a mark that generally is regarded as a slur against Asians, the Court explained, if a trademark registration bar is viewpoint based, it is unconstitutional.[23] Such a restriction "offends a bedrock First Amendment principle: Speech may not be banned on the ground that it expresses ideas that offend."[24] The Court then concluded that the registration prohibition was viewpoint based.[25] Consequently, the government must allow a musical group to trademark "Slants" even though that term is a racial slur of Asians.[26]

Third, in *Iancu v. Brunetti*, the Supreme Court reviewed the Patent and Trademark Office's refusal to register "FUCT" as a trademark.[27] As in *Matal*, the Court again determined Congress violated the Constitution when it prohibited the registration of "immoral" or "scandalous" trademarks.[28] The Court emphasized governmental agencies "may not discriminate against speech based on the ideas or opinions it conveys."[29] Because the law "allows registration of marks when their messages accord with, but not when their messages defy, society's sense of decency or propriety," the "statute, on its face, distinguishes between two opposed sets of ideas: those aligned with conventional moral standards and those hostile to them; those inducing societal nods of approval and those provoking offense and condemnation."[30] Consequently, the Court refused to allow the government to enforce the statute barring such registrations.[31]

B. Exceptions to the Freedom of Speech

The Freedom of Speech is not absolute. There are a "few categories of speech that the government can regulate or punish."[32] Even so, "new categories of unprotected speech may not be added to the list by a legislature that concludes certain speech is too harmful to be tolerated."[33] Only the Supreme Court can create exceptions. The Court has refused to recognize categorical exclusions for depictions of animal cruelty[34] and depictions of violence to children,[35] but it has declared that some categories of expression are beyond the protection of the Freedom of Speech. Those exceptions with applicability to public colleges and universities are discussed below.

1. Incitement

Incitement is limited to advocacy "directed to inciting or producing imminent lawless action and is likely to incite or produce such action."[36] There are two requirements. First, the lawless action must be imminent. A call for lawless action at some future time is insufficient. Second, even if a call for lawless action is imminent, there must be a likelihood of the speech producing the lawless action.

2. Threat

The Supreme Court's definition of threat "encompass those statements where the speaker means to communicate a serious expression of an intent to commit an act of unlawful violence to a particular individual or group of individuals."[37] To be considered a threat, the speaker must intend to actually make an actual threat or act with knowledge that the communication will be viewed as a threat.[38]

3. Defamation

Defamation is an intentional "false written or oral statement that damages another's reputation."[39] One commits defamation by inflicting "malicious or groundless harm to the reputation or good name of another by the making of a false statement to a third person."[40] Defamation in written form is called "libel" and defamation in oral form is called "slander."[41]

At the time of the First Amendment's adoption, defamation "of an individual was a common-law crime, and thus criminal in the colonies. Indeed, at common law, truth or good motives was no defense."[42] Consequently, defamation is outside the scope of the Freedom of Speech.[43]

The Court has narrowed the scope of defamation for "public figures," those who are placed in positions of prominence either voluntarily, such as through their jobs as public officials, or unwillingly, such as when they are thrust into the public consciousness as a result of having been involved in matters of public interest.[44] With public figures, liability for defamation occurs only if the speaker or writer acts with "actual malice," which means a reckless disregard for whether the statement is true.[45] In other words, the standard for defaming an ordinary person is simply a false statement which damages the ordinary person's reputation, but the standard for defaming a political leader or celebrity requires both the false statement and a reckless disregard for the truth.

4. Fighting Words

In the 1942 case of *Chaplinsky v. New Hampshire*, the Supreme Court ruled that "fighting words" were categorically excluded from the Freedom of Speech.[46] The Court defined "fighting words" as "those personally abusive epithets which, when addressed to the ordinary citizen, are, as a matter of common knowledge, inherently likely to provoke violent reaction."[47] While the Court has never repudiated *Chaplinsky* and continues to cite it regularly, the Court has never invalidated another statute or ordinance based on the "fighting words" exclusion.

5. Harassment

"There is no categorical 'harassment exception' to the First Amendment's free speech clause"[48] but the Supreme Court held that public school districts can incur monetary liability under Title IX for responding with deliberate indifference to one student's "harassment" of another student.[49] As such, by inference, expression that amounts to "harassment" under Title IX is not within the freedom of speech. Under Title IX, harassment is limited to expression or conduct so "severe, pervasive, and objectively offensive that it can be said to deprive the victims of access to the educational opportunities or benefits provided by the school."[50]

The definition of harassment of Title IX, which deals with education, is subtly different from the one under Title VII, which applies in most employment contexts. The Title VII standard covers expression or conduct so "severe or pervasive enough to create an objectively hostile or abusive work environment—an environment that a reasonable person would find hostile."[51] Although it is likely that the Supreme Court would find a public employer liable for expression that constitutes harassment under Title VII, the Court has never addressed whether the First Amendment protects expression that constitutes harassment under Title VII. To the extent that institutional policies impose broader definitions of harassment than the Title IX or Title VII, they may well violate the First Amendment.

To be sure, this analysis is limited to expression. Clearly, "non-expressive, physically harassing *conduct* is entirely outside the [scope] of the free speech clause."[52] "While drawing the line between speech and conduct can be difficult, [court] precedents have long drawn it, and the line is long familiar to the bar."[53]

C. Government May Not Compel Speech

Because the First Amendment protects "the right to speak freely and the right to refrain from speaking at all,"[54] the government "may not compel affirmance of a belief with which the speaker disagrees."[55] When the government tries to do so anyway, it violates this "cardinal constitutional command."[56] For example, government officials may not force residents to display a license plate conveying a message with which the residents disagree.[57] Similarly, the government may not force its employees to fund the speech of a labor union.[58]

D. Forum Analysis

The Constitution also requires public institutions to permit speech in a wide variety of locations. College and university policies often prohibit speech in particular areas of campus, but the constitutionality of those restrictions depends upon whether the area is a traditional public forum, designated public forum, limited public forum, or nonpublic forum. Each of these characterizations deserves further elaboration.

First, a traditional public forum is a space that has been "used for purposes of assembly, communicating thoughts between citizens and discussing public questions,"[59] such as a park or public town square. This means the policies of public institutions may impose speech restrictions "only when the exclusion is necessary to serve a compelling state interest and the exclusion is narrowly drawn to achieve that interest."[60] Stated differently, the government must be able to show that the restriction is designed to ensure public safety, or some equally important objective and the government must be able to show there is no other practical way to achieve that interest.

At the same time, in a traditional public forum, governmental entities "may impose reasonable restrictions on the time, place, or manner of protected speech, provided the restrictions are justified without reference to the content of the regulated speech, that they are narrowly tailored to serve a significant governmental interest, and that they leave open ample alternative channels for communication of the information."[61] For example, city officials may close a park between sunset and sunrise or prohibit open flames. Those restrictions must apply to everyone regardless of the viewpoints that people wish to express.

Second, officials of "a government entity may create 'a designated public forum' if government property that has not traditionally been regarded as a public forum is intentionally opened up for that purpose."[62] If a policy of a public college or university creates a designated public forum, then "restrictions on speech in a designated public forum are subject to the same strict scrutiny as restrictions in a traditional public forum."[63] "Government restrictions on speech in a designated public forum are subject to the same strict scrutiny as restrictions in a traditional public forum."[64]

Third, a limited public forum is a space that institutions have opened "for a limited purpose such as use by certain groups ... or for the discussion of certain subjects."[65] Examples of such spaces may include, for example, auditoriums reserved only for certain types of events; bulletin boards available only to a designated department's faculty and students, or for discussion of only specific subjects; display areas available to advertise only events sponsored by registered student organizations.

Regulation of expression in a limited public forum must be "reasonable in light of the purpose served by the forum and ... viewpoint neutral."[66] To illustrate, campus officials may allow student groups to post flyers about upcoming events on a bulletin board, but may prohibit outside groups from posting flyers. The rule ensures that the bulletin board is used for the purpose that the institution intended.

In *Pleasant Grove City v. Summum*,[67] the Supreme Court clarified "designated public fora" and "limited public fora" were not interchangeable terms for the same constitutional concept, but were in fact two separate constitutional concepts requiring different levels of scrutiny.[68] By doing so, the Justices resolved "the confusion over terminology and scrutiny levels [noticed by lower courts] after the Supreme Court first articulated the concept of a 'limited public forum.'"[69]

Unless an institution has specifically declared the existence of a limited public forum, the open spaces on campuses of public institutions likely will be characterized as "designated public fora."[70] The distinction is important because, as detailed above, it is much more difficult to justify restrictions in a designated public forum than in a limited public forum.

Finally, a nonpublic forum is property or spaces which are not open for the purpose of public expression, such as an administrative office. In a nonpublic forum, institutional policies may control or limit expression if "the regulation ... is reasonable and not an effort to suppress expression merely because public officials oppose the speaker's view."[71] For example, officials of a public college or university could adopt a policy prohibiting any expressive activities inside its administrative offices, within its classroom buildings, in its parking garages, or those areas used for healthcare activities.

Importantly then, institutional officials have discretion to choose if and how to use spaces and facilities for various degrees and types of expression. Clear communication of expectations and conditions about these various spaces, and consistent application across viewpoints is critical. In some instances, a State Legislature may remove this discretion and make the decision for the university. For example, Kentucky law provides the "generally accessible, open, outdoor areas of the campus be maintained as traditional public forums for students and faculty to express their views, so that the free expression of students and faculty is not limited to particular areas of the campus often described as 'free speech zones.'"[72]

E. Government Speech

The First Amendment restricts the ability of public institutions to regulate student speech, but the Constitution does not regulate government speech.[73] A state university has the right to "speak for itself"[74] and "is entitled to say what it wishes."[75] As a governmental agency, officials of a public college or university are "entitled to promote a program, to espouse a policy, or to take a position. In doing so, it represents its citizens, and it carries out its duties on their behalf."[76] Indeed, a campus policy is permitted "to regulate the content of what is or is not expressed when it is the speaker or when it enlists private entities to convey its own message."[77]

Consequently, while institutional officials may not be able to discipline students for their expression, they can condemn the student's expression and/or espouse their own views. Put another way, students have the right to espouse the views of Nazis or the Confederacy, but the institution does not have to remain neutral while the students do so. An institution can—and should—express its disagreement with speech that, in the judgment of the institution's leaders, contradicts the fundamental values of the university.

II. STUDENTS

Public college and university students, like their counterparts in K-12, do not "shed their constitutional rights to freedom of speech or expression," even at the university gate.[78] "The freedom to speak and the freedom to hear are inseparable; they are two sides of the same coin. But the coin itself is the process of thought and discussion."[79]

While institutional policies can certainly prevent a student from disrupting classroom instructions, courts "must be more skeptical of a school's efforts to regulate speech" outside of the classroom "for doing so may mean the student cannot engage in that kind of speech at all."[80] Indeed, campus officials "have an interest in protecting a student's unpopular expression."[81] "Our representative democracy only works if we protect the 'marketplace of ideas.' This free exchange facilitates an informed public opinion, which, when transmitted to lawmakers, helps produce laws that reflect the People's will."[82]

This part explores the specific rights of public higher education students including the right to be free from compelled speech in the education context as well as the rights of student organizations.

A. Public Colleges and Universities May Not Compel Students to Speak

As discussed above in Part I of this chapter, it is a core constitutional principle that government may not compel someone to speak. Nevertheless, officials at public institutions sometimes attempt to compel speech from their students. Many faculty members require their students to adopt specific assumptions, mandate students lobby for left-wing causes, are intolerant of those students who disagree with their views, evaluate their students' "dispositions," and punish their student writing assignments that make the faculty member uncomfortable.

Indeed, in some instances, students who aspire to be professionals are punished for failing to conform to professional norms.[83] More specifically, some professional groups, such as psychological counselors or social workers, impose ethical requirements on those who are part of the profession.[84] In some instances, these ethical requirements may require students to violate their faith or their conscience.[85]

In *National Institute of Family & Life Advocates v. Becerra*,[86] the Supreme Court ruled California's legislature violated the Constitution by requiring professionals, "to inform women how they can obtain state-subsidized abortions."[87] The constitutional challenge involved a group of professionals who were opposed to abortion and who actively tried to persuade women from pursuing abortion.[88] By compelling the professionals to speak a particular message, the Court found the government was "altering the content" of the professionals' speech.[89] Most significantly, the Court rejected the notion, embraced by some federal courts of appeal,[90] that strict scrutiny does not apply to content based regulation of "professional speech."[91] This aspect of the holding broadens the freedom of speech for professionals and aspiring professionals speaking in their professional context.

Faculty members and administrators may look to compel an affirmation of certain views, but *National Institute of Family & Life Advocates* reaffirms the State "must not be allowed to force persons to express a message contrary to their deepest convictions. Freedom of speech secures freedom of thought and belief."[92] Similarly, to the extent that public college and university administrators seek to punish speech of aspiring professionals for failing to adhere to professional norms, *National Institute of Family & Life Advocates'* rejection of lesser scrutiny for "professional speech" precludes such actions.

In sum, all members of public institutional communities are free from compulsion. Just as speech from professionals will be the same as speech from ordinary citizens for constitutional purposes, speech from those students who aspire to a particular profession must be treated the same as speech from ordinary students.

B. Student Organizations

Recognizing "the First Amendment rights of speech and association extend to the campuses of state universities," the Supreme Court has protected the Free Expression rights of student organizations.[93] Specifically, the Court has recognized a right of recognition,[94] a right of access to facilities,[95] a right of funding,[96] and, except in situations where officials have adopted an "all comers" policy, a right to exclude those who disagree with the organization's views and objectives.[97] Each of these rights warrants further discussion.

1. Recognition

The Constitution does not require public college and university officials to recognize student organizations, but if the university chooses to recognize student groups, there is a right of recognition.[98] As the Supreme Court explained in *Healey v. James*, the "mere disagreement . . . with the group's philosophy affords no reason to deny it recognition . . . The College, acting here as the instrumentality of the State, may not restrict speech or association . . ."[99]

As a practical matter, this means that *any* group of students can receive recognition. Undoubtedly, many of those groups will hold opposing views on politics, religion, abortion, sexual orientation, social justice, gun rights, and other hot button issues. The fact that a sizable portion, or even a majority, of the campus community vehemently disagree with a group is no basis for denying recognition. Nor is the fact some students feel "unsafe" being on campus with those who espouse opposing beliefs as a justification for denying recognition.

Institutional officials may not refuse recognition because of the student organization's viewpoints but they may require the student organization to (1) obey the campus rules; (2) refrain from disrupting classes; and (3) obey all applicable federal, state, and local laws.[100] As a practical matter, this means that institutional officials can impose some neutral criteria for recognition, such as having a faculty advisor, having a constitution, and having a specified number of members. Of course, institutional officials cannot deny recognition simply because the officials or a significant part of the campus community dislike the organization. Moreover, the administrators may not deny recognition because members of the organization at other campuses or in the outside community have engaged in conduct the officials deem unacceptable.[101]

To be sure, this mandate of viewpoint neutrality toward student organizations does not mean that college and university officials must compromise their own viewpoints. While the institution must accommodate the viewpoints of all student groups, "students and faculty are free to associate to voice their disapproval of the [student organization's] message."[102] If one on campus finds a particular viewpoint disagreeable, the solution is to promote an alternative viewpoint, not to suppress the disagreeable perspective. If college and university officials are going to express disapproval in the name of their institutions, they should make certain that they are authorized to speak for their schools. In fact, there likely will be situations where institutional governing boards have vastly different attitudes toward student organizations.

2. Access to Facilities

Recognized student groups often desire to use university facilities, such as vacant classrooms or spaces in the student residence halls or the student center. Like the right of recognition, college and university administrators are not constitutionally required to allow student organizations access to facilities. Yet, as the Supreme Court decided in *Widmar v. Vincent*, if officials choose to allow recognized student organizations to access facilities, then it must allow all recognized student organizations to access facilities on the same terms and conditions.[103]

Of course, administrators can deny access to groups other than recognized student groups. If institutional policy allows the public to access space, then the institution may well have established a designated public forum or a limited public forum.

3. Funding

Similarly, if officials at a public college or university decide to provide funding to student groups, then they cannot withhold funding simply because of disagreement with the group's viewpoint. In *Rosenberger v. Rector and Visitors of University of Virginia*, the Supreme Court found university officials could not withhold benefits from a student newspaper simply because of its perspective.[104]

Of course, if a student group has a right to receive funding, there is still the question of the source of the funding. Public colleges and universities often require all students to pay a student activity fee (a tax) and then proceeds of these fees are distributed to recognized student groups. In effect, a Democrat subsidizes the College Republicans, an atheist subsidizes the Christian groups, a Muslim subsidizes the Jewish students, and LGBTQIA+ students subsidize traditional marriage advocacy groups.

Such forced subsidies are constitutionally problematic. The Constitution protects the right "to refrain from speaking at all"[105] and the "right to eschew association for expressive purposes."[106] While the Supreme Court historically approved public employees' forced subsidy of labor unions,[107] in *Janus v. American Federation of State, County, & Municipal Employees, Council 31*,[108] the Court ended "the oddity of privileging compelled union support over compelled party support and [brought] a measure of greater coherence to our First Amendment law."[109]

"Forcing free and independent individuals to endorse ideas they find objectionable is always demeaning" and "[c]ompelling a person to *subsidize* the speech of other private speakers raises similar First Amendment concerns."[110] Therefore, any forced subsidy "violates the First Amendment and cannot continue" unless the individual "affirmatively consents to pay."[111] Simply put, forcing "individuals to mouth support for views they find objectionable violates that cardinal constitutional command, and in most contexts, any such effort would be universally condemned."[112]

Nevertheless, in *Board of Regents v. Southworth*, a case decided almost two decades before *Janus*, the Supreme Court explicitly upheld forced subsidies for student groups at public colleges and universities.[113] In reaching this result, the Court recognized the "avowed purpose" for recognizing student groups is "to provide a forum in which students can exchange ideas."[114] Indeed, student activity fees are designed to facilitate "the free and open exchange of ideas by, and among, its students"[115] and to "encourage a diversity of views from private speakers."[116]

Nevertheless, under *Southworth*, institutional officials must "provide some protection to its students' First Amendment interests."[117] Specifically, administrators "may not prefer some viewpoints to others . . . Viewpoint neutrality is the justification for requiring the student to pay the fee in the first instance and for ensuring the integrity of the program's operation once the funds have been collected."[118] The public institution must remain viewpoint neutral.[119]

Although *Southworth* remains binding precedent until overruled,[120] *Janus* appears to contradict *Southworth*. If employees cannot be forced to financially support the activities of a labor union with which they disagree, then it is difficult to see how students can be forced to financially support the activities of a student organization with which they disagree. The Supreme Court may revisit the constitutionality of forced subsidies through student activity fees.

4. Limited Freedom of Association

Recognized student organizations generally have a right to determine who qualifies for membership or leadership positions. "An individual's freedom to speak, to worship, and to petition the government for the redress of grievances could not be vigorously protected from interference by the State unless a correlative freedom to engage in group effort toward those ends were not also guaranteed."[121] "This right is crucial in preventing the majority from imposing its views on groups that would rather express other, perhaps unpopular, ideas."[122] "If the government were free to restrict individuals' ability to join together and speak, it could essentially silence views that the First Amendment is intended to protect."[123] This freedom of association "is not reserved for advocacy groups. But to come within its ambit, a group must engage in some form of expression, whether it be public or private."[124]

"Freedom of association . . . plainly presupposes a freedom not to associate."[125] "Freedom of association would prove an empty guarantee if associations could not limit control over their decisions to those who share the interests and persuasions that underlie the association's being."[126] "The forced inclusion of an unwanted person in a group infringes the group's freedom of expressive association if the presence of that person affects in a significant way the group's ability to advocate public or private viewpoints."[127]

Therefore, governmental officials, such as the public institutional administrators, may intrude on the freedom of association only "by regulations adopted to serve compelling state interests, unrelated to the suppression of ideas that cannot be achieved through means significantly less restrictive of associational freedoms."[128] For example, during the 1980's, the Supreme Court held that States' compelling interest in ending sex discrimination justified requiring the Jaycees[129] and the Rotary clubs to admit women.[130]

When controversies arise regarding the freedom of association, courts are required to "examine whether or not the application of the state law would impose any 'serious burden' on the organization's rights of expressive association."[131] Judges must "give deference to an association's assertions regarding the nature of its expression" and "to an association's view of what would impair its expression."[132] It is not necessary for an organization's core purpose to be expressive or for all members to agree with all aspects of the message.[133]

Under this framework, the Supreme Court has upheld statutes requiring civic organizations to admit women,[134] but has allowed both parade organizers[135] and the Boy Scouts to exclude individuals who are gays and lesbians.[136] The cases have turned on whether "the enforcement of these [policies]" would "materially interfere with the ideas that the organization sought to express."[137]

Despite the clarity of these cases, in *Christian Legal Society v. Martinez*, the Supreme Court upheld—as a matter of federal constitutional law—policies at public institutions requiring student groups to admit "all comers."[138] In other words, the College Democrats must admit Republicans, the LGBTQIA+ group must admit straight individuals who oppose LGBTQIA+ rights, the Chess Club must admit those who prefer checkers, the Red Sox fan club must admit Yankee supporters, and, most significantly, religious groups must admit those who disagree with the faith.

Under the reasoning of *Christian Legal Society*, as a condition of becoming recognized student organizations, a status affording them such benefits as access to campus facilities and some funding, student groups must admit "all comers," including those who disagree with their deeply held beliefs and values.[139]

While nothing in the Supreme Court's opinion limits *Christian Legal Society* to a particular context, the reality is the case arose in an unusual factual situation. Although most public institutions allow student groups to exclude those who disagree with the group's objectives or do not share the group's interests, *Christian Legal Society* involved a policy forbidding any student organization from discriminating for any reason. Under this "all-comers policy," the Young Democrats had to allow Republicans to join; the Vegetarian Society had to include carnivores; and the Chess Club had to allow members who would prefer to play checkers.

If institutions allow some student political organizations or student special interest organizations to exclude those who do not share the group's ideology or interests, values, then it will be difficult for those officials to justify forcing student religious groups to admit nonbelievers.

III. ALL EMPLOYEES MAY SPEAK AS PRIVATE CITIZENS ON ISSUES OF PUBLIC CONCERN

Public higher education faculty, administrators, and staff "do not surrender their First Amendment rights by accepting public employment."[140] Indeed, "the First Amendment protects a public employee's right, in certain circumstances, to speak as a citizen addressing matters of public concern."[141]

As *Garcetti v. Ceballos* made clear, there is no constitutional protection when employees "make statements pursuant to their official duties."[142] In determining the scope of an employee's free speech rights, "the critical question is whether the speech at issue is itself ordinarily within the scope of an employee's duties, not whether it merely concerns those duties."[143] In answering that question, the courts largely ignore job description and focus on practical considerations.[144]

If an employee speaks as a private citizen, then a court must evaluate whether the employee's speech involves a matter of public concern. Speech involves matters of public concern "when it can 'be fairly considered as relating to any matter of political, social, or other concern to the community,' or when it 'is a subject of legitimate news interest; that is, a subject of general interest and of value and concern to the public.'"[145]

Finally, if public college or university employees speaking as citizens and if the speech is on matters of public concern, courts must strike "a balance between the interests of the [employee], as a citizen, in commenting upon matters of public concern and the interest of the State, as an employer, in promoting the efficiency of the public services it performs through its employees."[146]

IV. ACADEMIC FREEDOM

"Our Nation is deeply committed to safeguarding academic freedom, which is of transcendent value to all of us and not merely to the teachers concerned. That freedom is therefore a special concern of the First Amendment."[147] "Teachers and students must always remain free to inquire, to study and to evaluate, to gain new maturity and understanding; otherwise our civilization will stagnate and die."[148]

As the *Chicago Statement*, the leading contemporary statement of academic freedom, explains, "the ideas of different members of the University community will often and quite naturally conflict," but institutional officials should not "attempt to shield individuals from ideas and opinions they find unwelcome, disagreeable, or even deeply offensive."[149] Faculty members must be able to criticize the Supreme Court's jurisprudence as unduly *restrictive*[150] or overly *permissive* of racial preferences.[151] Researchers in the academy must be able to argue affirmative action actually hurts those students admitted through such programs[152] or should be expanded to include students from high poverty backgrounds.[153] Indeed, "concerns about civility and mutual respect can never be used as a justification for closing off discussion of ideas, however offensive or disagreeable those ideas may be to some" individuals.[154]

Yet, "fitting academic freedom within the rubric of the first amendment is in many respects an extremely difficult challenge. The term is nowhere mentioned in the text of the first amendment. It is inconceivable that those who debated and ratified the first amendment thought about academic freedom."[155] Consequently, "'academic freedom' is a term that is often used, but little explained, by federal courts."[156] In particular, confusion exists as to the exact scope of academic freedom.[157]

A. Constitutional Definition

On the one hand, there is a constitutional definition.[158] As discussed earlier in this chapter, students, nonfaculty employees, and faculty members at public colleges and universities have broad First Amendment rights. Thus, "*all* members of the [public college or university] community [have] the broadest possible latitude to speak, write, listen, challenge, and learn" and "to discuss any problem that presents itself."[159] Every public institution must have a "commitment to free expression and free inquiry. All views, beliefs, and perspectives deserve to be articulated free from interference. This commitment underpins every part of [public higher education's] mission."[160]

In this constitutional sense, academic freedom is not limited to the faculty, but extends to students, nonfaculty scientists and researchers, and even administrators. These individuals frequently make significant scholarly contributions. For example, law students—through student written law review notes and case comments—can help to shape the law. At major research institutions, staff researchers often author more papers than their faculty counterparts. Administrators, many of whom had significant scholarly and policy accomplishments before assuming their current roles, continue to publish extensively. Under the constitutional definition, if one is part of the public college or university community, one enjoys academic freedom.

B. Professional Definition

On the other hand, there is a professional definition of academic freedom.[161] The American Association of University Professors ("AAUP") "conceived academic freedom as a professional norm, not a legal one" and "justified academic freedom on the basis of its social utility as a means of advancing the search for truth, rather than its status as a manifestation of First Amendment rights."[162] Simply put, it was the "professional norms of the academy, which are in turn grounded in custom and usage,"[163] not the Constitution, which provides the substance of the professional definition.[164]

The professional definition of academic freedom is narrower than the constitutional definition. The German notion of academic freedom, which inspired the AAUP, includes both a freedom of faculty to teach as they see fit ("lehrfreiheit") and a freedom of students to learn ("lernfreiheit").[165] In this sense, the German notion resembles the constitutional definition of everyone having academic freedom. Surprisingly, when AAUP first articulated the professional definition of academic freedom in 1915[166] it explicitly dropped the students' freedom to learn ("lernfreiheit").[167] The organization "has always assumed that student freedom is not an integral part of academic freedom, but is something different—and something less."[168] The AAUP's focus is exclusively on the rights of the faculty members.[169]

C. The Constitutional and Professional Definition Are Not Synonymous

Because of the differences in scope, the constitutional and professional definitions of academic freedom "are seriously incompatible and probably ultimately irreconcilable."[170] Even so, it is conventional wisdom[171] among public higher education faculty that the constitutional and professional definitions are synonymous.[172] Many faculty members believe "every professor possesses a constitutional right to determine for himself, without the input of the university (and perhaps even contrary to the university's desires), the subjects of his research, writing, and teaching."[173] In short, these faculty members believe they have a special "constitutional right enjoyed by only a limited class of citizens."[174]

The faculty members' conventional wisdom is wrong. The AAUP professional definition is not part of our constitutional fabric. To say otherwise "asks the courts to treat publicly employed academics differently from all other classes of public employees" and "requires the courts to designate scholarly and classroom speech as uniquely valuable, as compared with the job-required speech of nonacademic public employees, and even the nonacademic speech of academic public employees."[175] Such a result betrays the "the bedrock of all First Amendment protection"—the emphasis "on the prevention of content and viewpoint discrimination, as well as discrimination against particular speakers."[176]

V. THE TEACHING/RESEARCH EXCEPTION TO *GARCETTI*

While the Constitution does not adopt the AAUP professional definition of academic freedom, faculty members speech in classrooms or in the context of their research may well receive different constitutional scrutiny than the on-the-job speech of public employees.

As discussed above in the section on employee speech, in *Garcetti*,[177] the Supreme Court declared that a public employee's speech pursuant to their official duties is not constitutionally protected.[178] Still, it is unclear "whether the First Amendment protects faculty from reprisals by their institutions for speech within the duties of their job."[179] *Garcetti* "may not have directly imperiled speech rights, but it may have done something worse—left academics and school teachers in a troubling state of uncertainty about their rights."[180]

Justice Souter, in dissent, expressed "hope that today's majority does not mean to imperil First Amendment protection of academic freedom in public colleges and universities, whose teachers necessarily speak and write pursuant to . . . official duties."[181] Yet, the Court explicitly declined to address whether "the analysis we conduct today would apply in the same manner to a case involving speech related to scholarship or teaching."[182]

The Supreme Court's refusal to say whether *Garcetti* applies to a faculty member's academic speech may be an implicit suggestion that *Garcetti* does not apply and can also be viewed as an implicit endorsement of the view that

Garcetti does not apply to academic speech within the classroom or during research.[183] Conversely, the court's refusal may be an implicit acknowledgment of the differences between faculty members, who have a large amount of autonomy, and public employees who refuse to carry out their supervisors' instructions, which was the situation in *Garcetti*. Ultimately, the Supreme Court itself may have to decide.

Of course, there are important policy reasons for saying *Garcetti* should not apply to academic speech.[184] First, because "democracy and speech, including academic speech, assist one another," faculty with "expertise within their given fields can aid popular representatives in reaching decisions and in shaping an informed response to rapid change."[185] Second, because most private institutions, through contract or policy, extend a large degree of individual academic freedom, faculty members will simply leave if they feel the public institution is overly regulating their activities.[186] Third, if there is no exception to *Garcetti* for teaching and scholarship, then "the academic speech of public university professors is among the *least protected forms of speech*."[187] "[A]cademic speech is indisputably high-value speech, but in the public university workplace, it qualifies for the same protection as indisputably low-value speech—no protection."[188]

Given the Supreme Court's previous pronouncements about the importance of academic discourse, all of the lower appellate courts to consider the issue have recognized an exception to *Garcetti* for a faculty member's speech in the classroom or in academic research.[189] As the Sixth Circuit explained, "the academic-freedom exception to *Garcetti* covers all classroom speech related to matters of public concern, whether that speech is germane to the contents of the lecture or not. The need for the free exchange of ideas in the college classroom is unlike that in other public workplace settings."[190] More specifically, officials in public higher education "cannot force professors to avoid controversial viewpoints altogether in deference to a state-mandated orthodoxy."[191]

While the lower federal appellate courts have universally recognized an exception to *Garcetti* for teaching and academic research, the exact scope of this exception is likely narrow. Faculty members must adhere to "professional norms" in their classroom expression or academic research.[192] For example, astronomy faculty members should not teach their students that the moon is made of green cheese or author research papers defending such a proposition.[193] If faculty members defy these professional norms, they may find that the *Garcetti* exception does not apply.

At the same time, the exception to *Garcetti* likely does not extend to those aspects of faculty members' responsibilities that do not involve teaching or scholarship. When faculty members perform administrative work, serve on an institutional committee, or represent their institution in a nonacademic setting, then the faculty members' expression logically should receive the same treatment as the speech of any other public employee. Similarly, faculty members, like other employees, must adhere to the institutional policies regarding procurement, use of equipment, and approvals for outside employment.

Of course, even if the teaching and scholarship exception to *Garcetti* applies and a faculty member's expression is private citizen speech, the constitutional analysis does not end. As discussed in Part III of this chapter, even if a public employee is speaking as a private citizen, then a court must determine whether the employee's speech involves a matter of public concern.[194] If it does involve a matter of public concern, then courts must "strike a balance between the interests of the [employee], as a citizen, in commenting upon matters of public concern and the interest of the State, as an employer, in promoting the efficiency of the public services it performs through its employees."[195]

V. SUMMARY OF MAJOR CASES IN THIS CHAPTER

Adams v. Trustees of the University of North Carolina-Wilmington, 640 F.3d 550 (4th Cir. 2011)

The Fourth Circuit decided there is an exception to *Garcetti* for a faculty member's speech in the context of teaching and research. Consequently, the appellate court reversed a ruling in favor of the university on a First Amendment claim and remanded for further consideration.

Buchanan v. Alexander, 919 F.3d 847 (5th Cir. 2019)

The Fifth Circuit determined there is an exception to *Garcetti* for a faculty member's speech in the context of teaching and research. Accordingly, university officials in Louisiana did not violate the rights of a dismissed former faculty member who used profanity in discussing her sex life and that of her students in class because her speech was not on a matter of public concern such that the university's sexual harassment policy did not violate her First Amendment rights.

Board of Regents of University of Wisconsin System v. Southworth, 529 U.S. 217 (2000)

The Supreme Court held a state university could impose a mandatory student fee and then use the proceeds of that fee to fund student organizations.

However, if the institution does so, it must allocate funds in a viewpoint neutral manner.

Christian Legal Society v. Martinez, 561 U.S. 661 (2010)

The Supreme Court found a public university may require recognized student organizations to admit "all comers" as a condition of recognition. Consequently, a student religious group was required to admit students who disagreed with its beliefs.

Demers v. Austin, 746 F.3d 402 (9th Cir. 2014)

The Ninth Circuit ruled that there is an exception to *Garcetti* for a faculty member's speech in the context of teaching and research. Nevertheless, because the law was not clearly established, the administrators were entitled to qualified immunity on the Freedom of Speech issue.

Garcetti v. Ceballos, 547 U.S. 410 (2006)

The Supreme Court concluded the First Amendment does not protect the free speech rights of public employees who engage in speech while acting in their official capacities.

Healy v. James, 408 U.S. 169 (1972)

The Supreme Court determined campus officials could not deny a student group recognition based on their disagreement with its positions, unsupported fears that it would have been disruptive, and its assumed association with a larger national body. The case is significant in establishing the right of student groups to achieve recognition on a neutral basis.

Iancu v. Brunetti, 139 S. Ct. 2294 (2019)

The Supreme Court found the Lanham Act's bar on the registration of "immoral" or "scandalous" trademarks discriminates based on viewpoint, violated the Freedom of Speech.

Keyishian v. Board of Regents of University of State of New York, 385 U.S. 589 (1967)

The Supreme Court invalidated statutory provisions from New York banning public employment for individuals who engaged in "subversive" activity as unconstitutionally vague.

Mahanoy Area School District v. B. L, 141 S. Ct. 2038 (2021)

The Supreme Court ruled school officials in Pennsylvania violated a student's First Amendment rights when they suspended her from a cheerleading team for posting a vulgar, off-campus message on her Snapchat account.

Matal v. Tam, 137 S. Ct. 1744 (2017)

The Supreme Court invalidated the disparagement clause of the Lanham Act, which prohibited federal trademark registration for marks that might disparage any persons, living or dead, as facially invalid.

Meriwether v. Hartop, 992 F.3d 492 (6th Cir. 2021)

The Sixth Circuit decided there is an exception to *Garcetti* for a faculty member's speech in the context of teaching and research. Therefore, a faculty member in Ohio demonstrated that because his refusal to use an individual's preferred pronouns during class, a core activity of teaching, involved a matter of public concern, he plausibly stated a First Amendment claim that his speech was entitled to protection. He also established a plausible claim that the underlying policy was not religiously neutral.

National Institute of Family Life Advocates v. Becerra, 138 S. Ct. 2361 (2018)

The Supreme Court found the Freedom of Speech prevented the State from compelling private persons to speak in a specific way. Consequently, the Court invalidated a California law mandating that crisis pregnancy centers provide notices about publicly funded family-planning services, including contraception and abortions.

Rosenberger v. Rector and Visitors of University of Virginia, 515 U.S. 819 (1995)

The Supreme Court ruled if university officials decided to fund student publications, then the officials could not deny funding to a Christian publication. The case is significant both for preventing viewpoint discrimination and finding funding of a religious message does not violate the Establishment Clause.

Rumsfeld v. Forum for Academic & Institutional Rights, 547 U.S. 47 (2006)

The Supreme Court ruled the federal government could require colleges and universities which receive federal funds to allow military recruiters on campus. The case is significant for the ability to force institutions to compromise academic freedom as a condition of receiving federal funds.

Snyder v. Phelps, 562 U.S. 443 (2011)

The Supreme Court concluded speech about same-sex activity made at a military funeral was protected by the Freedom of Speech. Therefore, the Court vacated the civil recovery for intentional inflection of emotional distress.

Sweezy v. New Hampshire, 354 U.S. 234 (1957)

The Supreme Court ruled state university officials could not punish a speaker on a university campus for refusing to answer questions about whether he was engaged in subversive activities because the inquiries violated his rights to academic freedom and political expression. The case is significant for its discussion of the importance of both individual and institutional academic freedom.

Widmar v. Vincent, 454 U.S. 263 (1981)

The Supreme Court decided when officials at a state university made facilities generally available for activities of registered student groups, they could not prevent faith-based organizations from gathering due to the religious content of their speech.

NOTES

1. *West Virginia State Board of Education v. Barnette*, 319 U.S. 624, 642 (1943).

2. *Sweezy v. New Hampshire*, 354 U.S. 234, 250 (1957).
3. *Speech First, Inc. v. Schlissel*, 939 F.3d 756, 761 (6th Cir. 2019).
4. Thomas Jefferson, *Letter to William Roscoe* (December 27, 1820). Available at https://founders.archives.gov/documents/Jefferson/98-01-02-1712.
5. Robert C. Post, DEMOCRACY, EXPERTISE, AND ACADEMIC FREEDOM: A FIRST AMENDMENT JURISPRUDENCE FOR THE MODERN STATE 64 (2012).
6. Greg Lukianoff & Jonathon Haidt, THE CODDLING OF THE AMERICAN MIND: HOW GOOD INTENTIONS AND BAD IDEAS ARE SETTING UP A GENERATION FOR FAILURE, 32–51 (2018).
7. *See* Heather MacDonald, THE DIVERSITY DELUSION: HOW RACE AND GENDER PANDERING CORRUPT THE UNIVERSITY AND UNDERMINE OUR CULTURE (2018).
8. *See* John D. Inazu, A CONFIDENT PLURALISM: SURVIVING AND THRIVING THROUGH DEEP DIFFERENCE (2016).
9. John Inazu, *The Purpose (and Limits) of the University*, 2018 UTAH L. REV. 943, 947 (2018).
10. Keith E. Whittington, SPEAK FREELY: WHY UNIVERSITIES MUST DEFEND FREE SPEECH 29 (2018).
11. Greg Lukianoff & Adam Goldstein, *Law Alone Can't Protect Free Speech*, WALL STREET JOURNAL (August 13, 2020).
12. The University of Chicago's Statement on Freedom of Expression (2015).
13. *Barnette*, 319 U.S. at 638.
14. *Matal v. Tam*, 137 S. Ct. 1744, 1765 (2017) (Kennedy, J., joined by Ginsburg, Sotomayor, & Kagan, JJ., concurring).
15. *United States v. Stevens*, 559 U.S. 460, 470 (2010) (citations omitted).
16. *Snyder v. Phelps*, 562 U.S. 443 (2011).
17. *Id.* at 453–59.
18. *Id.* at 455.
19. *Id.* at 454–57.
20. *Id.* at 458.
21. *Matal v. Tam*, 137 S. Ct. 1744 (2017).
22. 15 U.S.C. § 1052(a).
23. *Matal*, 137 S. Ct at 1761–62 (Alito, J., announcing the judgment of the Court); *Id.* at 1765–66 (Kennedy, J.).
24. *Id.* at 1751.
25. *Id.* at 1762–63 (Alito, J., announcing the judgment of the Court); *Id.* at 1765–66 (Kennedy, J., concurring).
26. *Id.* at 1762–63 (Alito, J., announcing the judgment of the Court); *Id.* at 1765–66 (Kennedy, J., concurring).
27. *Iancu v. Brunetti*, 139 S. Ct. 2294 (2019).
28. *Id.* at 2302.
29. *Id.* at 2299.
30. *Id.*
31. *Id.* at 2300.
32. *Matal*, 137 S. Ct. at 1765 (Kennedy, J., joined by Ginsburg, Sotomayor, & Kagan, JJ., concurring).

33. *Brown v. Entertainment Merchants Association*, 564 U.S. 786, 791(2011).
34. *Stevens*, 559 U.S. at 472.
35. *Brown*, 564 U.S. at 799.
36. *Brandenburg v. Ohio*, 395 U.S. 444, 447 (1969) *(per curiam)*.
37. *Virginia v. Black*, 538 U.S. 343, 359 (2003).
38. *Elonis v. United States*, 575 U.S. 723, 740 (2015).
39. BLACK's LAW DICTIONARY (11th ed. 2019).
40. *Id*.
41. *Id*.
42. *Beauharnais v. Illinois*, 343 U.S. 250, 254 (1952).
43. *Id.* at 255–57.
44. *New York Times v. Sullivan*, 376 U.S. 254, 279–80 (1964).
45. *Id.*
46. *Chaplinsky v. New Hampshire*, 315 U.S. 568, 572 (1942).
47. *Id.*
48. *Saxe v. State College Area School District.* 240 F.3d 200, 204 (3rd Cir. 2001) (Alito, J.).
49. *Davis v. Monroe County. Board of Education*, 526 U.S. 629, 650 (1999).
50. *Id.* at 650.
51. *Harris v. Forklift Systems, Inc.*, 510 U.S. 17, 21, (1993).
52. *Saxe*, 240 F.3d at 206.
53. *National Institute of Family & Life Advocates v. Becerra*, 138 S. Ct. 2361, 2373 (2018).
54. *Wooley v. Maynard,* 430 U.S. 705, 714 (1977).
55. *Hurley v. Irish-American Gay, Lesbian & Bisexual Group of Boston*, 515 U.S. 557, 573 (1995).
56. *Janus v. American Federation of State, County. & Municipal. Employees, Council 31*, 138 S. Ct. 2448, 2463 (2018).
57. *Wooley,* 430 U.S. at 714.
58. *Hurley,* 515 U.S. at 573.
59. *Perry Education Association v. Perry Local Educators' Association*, 460 U.S. 37, 45 (1983).
60. *Cornelius v. NAACP Legal Defense & Educational Fund, Inc.*, 473 U.S. 788, 800 (1985).
61. *Ward v. Rock Against Racism*, 491 U.S. 781, 791(1989).
62. *Pleasant Grove City, Utah v. Summum*, 555 U.S. 460, 469 (2009).
63. *Id.* at 470.
64. *Id.* at 469–70.
65. *Perry,* 460 U.S. at 45 n. 7 (internal citations omitted).
66. *Cornelius,* 473 U.S. at 806 (1985).
67. *Summum,* 555 U.S. at 469.
68. *Id.*
69. *Miller v. City of Cincinnati*, 622 F.3d 524, 535 n. 1 (6th Cir. 2010).
70. *See McGlone v. Bell,* 681 F.3d 718, 733 (6th Cir. 2012); *Hays County Guardian v. Supple,* 969 F.2d 111, 116 (5th Cir.1992).

71. *Perry*, 460 U.S. at 46.
72. Ky. Rev. Stat. 164.348(2)(j).
73. *Johanns v. Livestock Marketing Association*, 544 U.S. 550, 553 (2005).
74. *Board of Regents of the University of Wisconsin System v. Southworth*, 529 U.S. 217, 229 (2000).
75. *Rosenberger v. Rector and Visitors of University of Virginia*, 515 U.S. 819, 833 (1995).
76. *Walker v. Texas Division, Sons of Confederate Veterans, Inc.*, 576 U.S. 200, 208 (2015).
77. *Rosenberger*, 515 at 833.
78. *Tinker v. Des Moines Independent School District* 393 U.S. 503, 506 (1969).
79. *Kleindienst v. Mandel*, 408 U.S. 753, 775 (1972) (Marshall, J., dissenting).
80. *Mahanoy Area School District v. B. L*, 141 S. Ct. 2038, 2046 (2021).
81. *Id.*
82. *Id.*
83. *Keefe v. Adams*, 840 F.3d 523, 533 (8th Cir. 2016).
84. Todd A. DeMitchell, David T. Herbert, & Loan T. Phan, *The University Curriculum and the Constitution: Personal Beliefs and Professional Ethics in Graduate School Counseling Programs*, 39 J.C. & U.L. 303, 304–05 (2013).
85. *Id.* at 305.
86. 138 S. Ct. 2361 (2018).
87. *Id.* at 2371.
88. *Id.* at 2370.
89. *Id.* at 2371.
90. *King v. Governor of New Jersey*, 767 F.3d 216, 232 (3rd Cir. 2014); *Pickup v. Brown*, 740 F.3d 1208, 1227–1229 (9th Cir. 2014); *Moore–King v. County of Chesterfield*, 708 F.3d 560, 568–570 (4th Cir. 2013).
91. *National Institute of Family & Life Advocates*, 138 S. Ct. at 2371–75.
92. *Id.* at 2379 (Kennedy, joined by Roberts, C.J., Thomas, Alito, & Gorsuch, JJ., concurring).
93. *Widmar v. Vincent*, 454 U.S. 263, 269 (1981).
94. *Healey v. James*, 408 U.S. 169 (1972).
95. *Widmar*, 454 U.S. at 267–70.
96. *Rosenberger*, 515 U.S. at 829.
97. *Christian Legal Society v. Martinez*, 561 U.S. 661 (2010).
98. William A. Kaplin, Barbara A. Lee, Neal H. Hutchens, & Jacob H. Rooksby, THE LAW OF HIGHER EDUCATION 1373 (6th ed. 2020).
99. *Healy*, 408 U.S. at 187–88.
100. Kaplin, Lee, Hutchens, & Rooksby, *supra* note 98, at 1374–75.
101. *Healy*, 408 U.S. at 185–86.
102. *Rumsfeld v. Forum for Academic & Institutional Rights*, 547 U.S. 47, 69–70 (2006).
103. *Widmar*, 454 U.S. at 267–70.
104. *Rosenberger*, 515 U.S. at 829.
105. *Wooley*, 430 U.S. at 714.

106. *Roberts v. United States Jaycees,* 468 U.S. 609, 623 (1984).
107. *Abood v. Detroit Board of Education,* 431 U.S. 209 (1977).
108. *Janus,* 138 S. Ct. at 2484.
109. *Id.*
110. *Id.* at 2464.
111. *Id.* at 2486.
112. *Id. at* 2463.
113. *Southworth,* 529 U.S. at 233–34.
114. *Widmar,* 454 U.S. at 272 n.10.
115. *Southworth,* 529 U.S. at 229.
116. *Rosenberger,* 515 U.S. at 834.
117. *Southworth,* 529 U.S. at 233.
118. *Id.* at 233–34.
119. *Id.*
120. *Agostini v. Felton,* 521 U.S. 203, 237–38 (1997).
121. *Roberts,* 468 U.S. at 622.
122. *Boy Scouts of America v. Dale,* 530 U.S. 640, 647–48 (2000).
123. *Rumsfeld,* 547 U.S. at 68.
124. *Dale,* 530 U.S. at 648.
125. *Roberts,* 468 U.S. at 623.
126. *Democratic Party of U.S. v. Wisconsin ex rel. LaFollette,* 450 U.S. 107, 122 n.22 (1981).
127. *Dale,* 530 U.S. at 648.
128. *Roberts,* 468 U.S. at 623.
129. *Id.*
130. *Board of Directors of Rotary International v. Rotary Club of Duarte,* 481 U.S. 537, 549 (1987).
131. *Dale,* 530 U.S. at 685.
132. *Id.* at 653.
133. *Id.* at 655.
134. *Rotary Club,* 481 U.S. at 546–47.
135. *Hurley,* 515 U.S. at 572–73.
136. *Dale,* 530 U.S. at 655–60.
137. *Id.,* 530 U.S. at 657.
138. *Christian Legal Society,* 561 U.S. at 668.
139. *Id.*
140. *Lane v. Franks,* 573 U.S. 228, 231 (2014).
141. *Garcetti v. Cabellos,* 547 U.S. 410, 417 (2006).
142. *Id.* at 421.
143. *Lane,* 573 U.S. at 240.
144. *Garcetti,* 547 U.S. at 424–25.
145. *Lane,* 573 U.S. at 241.
146. *Pickering v. Board of Education of Township High School District 205, Will County,* 391 U.S. 563, 568, 11 (1968).

147. *Keyishian v. Board of Regents of University of State of New York*, 385 U.S. 589, 603 (1967).

148. *Sweezy*, 354 U.S. at 250.

149. Chicago Statement, *supra* note 12.

150. Randall Kennedy, For Discrimination: Race, Affirmative Action, & the Law (2013).

151. Russell K. Nieli, Wounds That Will Not Heal: Affirmative Action and Our Continuing Racial Divide (2012).

152. Richard Sander & Stuart Taylor, Jr., Mismatch: How Affirmative Action Hurts Students Its Intended to Help and Why Universities Won't Admit It (2012).

153. Sheryll Cashin, Place Not Race: A New Vision Of Opportunity In America (2014).

154. Chicago Statement, *supra* note 12.

155. David M. Rabban, *Functional Analysis of "Individual" and "Institutional" Academic Freedom Under the First Amendment*, 53 Law & Contemp. Probs. 227, 237 (1990) (cleaned up).

156. *Urofsky v. Gilmore*, 216 F.3d 401, 409 (4th Cir. 2000) (en banc).

157. *See* Stanley Fish, Versions of Academic Freedom: From Professionalism to Revolution (2014).

158. Walter P. Metzger, *Profession and Constitution: Two Definitions of Academic Freedom in America*, 66 Tex. L. Rev. 1265, 1267 (1988).

159. Chicago Statement, *supra* note 12.

160. University of Virginia, Statement of the Committee on Free Expression and Free Inquiry (2021).

161. Metzger, *supra* note 158, at 1267.

162. *Urofsky*, 216 F.3d at 411.

163. Kaplin, Lee, Hutchens, & Rooksby, *supra* note 98, at 753.

164. American Association of University Professors, Statement of Principles on Academic Freedom and Tenure (1940).

165. Richard Hofstadter & Walter P. Metzger, The Development of Academic Freedom in the United States, 386–91 (1955).

166. American Association of University Professors, Declaration of Principles (1915).

167. Metzger, *supra* note 158, at 1271–72.

168. *Id.* at 1272.

169. American Association of University Professors, Statement of Principles on Academic Freedom and Tenure (1940).

170. Metzger, *supra* note 158, at 1267.

171. Matthew W. Finkin, *Intramural Speech, Academic Freedom, and the First Amendment*, 66 Tex. L. Rev. 1323, 1324 (1988).

172. Scott R. Bauries, *Individual Academic Freedom: An Ordinary Concern of the First Amendment*, 83 Miss. L. 677, 678 (2014).

173. *Urofsky v. Gilmore*, 216 F.3d 401, 409–410 (4th Cir. 2000) (en banc).

174. *Id.* at 412.

175. Bauries, *supra* note 172, at 731.

176. *Id.* at 729–30.

177. *Garcetti*, 547 U.S. at 421.

178. *Id.*

179. J. Peter Byrne, *Neo-Orthodoxy in Academic Freedom,* 88 TEX. L. REV. 143, 163–64 (2009) (Reviewing Matthew W. Finkin & Robert C. Post, FOR THE COMMON GOOD: PRINCIPLES OF AMERICAN ACADEMIC FREEDOM (2009) & Stanley Fish, SAVE THE WORLD ON YOUR OWN TIME (2008)).

180. Scott R. Bauries & Patrick Schach, *Coloring Outside the Lines: Garcetti v. Ceballos in the Federal Appellate Courts*, 262 EDUCATION LAW REP. 357, 388 (2011).

181. *Garcetti*, 547 U.S. at 438 (Souter, J., dissenting).

182. *Garcetti,* 547 U.S. at 425.

183. Bauries & Schach, *supra* note 180, at 388–89.

184. *Urofsky,* 216 F.3d *at* 425 (Luttig, J., concurring); *Id.* 434–35 (Wilkinson, J., concurring).

185. *Id.* at 434–35 (Wilkinson, J., concurring) (cleaned up).

186. *Id.* at 425 (Luttig, J., concurring).

187. Bauries, *supra* note 172, at 715 (emphasis original).

188. *Id.*

189. *Meriwether v. Hartop*, 992 F.3d 492, (6th Cir. 2021); *Buchanan v. Alexander*, 919 F.3d 847, (5th Cir. 2019); *Demers v. Austin,* 746 F.3d 402 (9th Cir. 2014); *Adams v. Trustees of the University of N.C.-Wilmington*, 640 F.3d 550 (4th Cir. 2011).

190. *Meriwether*, 992 F.3d at 507.

191. *Id.* at 507.

192. Post, *supra* note 5, at 76.

193. *Id.* at 76–77.

194. *Lane*, 573 U.S. at 241.

195. *Pickering*, 391 U.S. at 568.

Chapter 2

The First Freedom

Religious Liberty on Campus

In far too many places, for far too long, our first freedom has fallen on deaf ears.—Justice Gorsuch[1]

"We are a religious people whose institutions presuppose a Supreme Being."[2] "The fact that the Founding Fathers believed devotedly that there was a God and that the unalienable rights of man were rooted in Him is clearly evidenced in their writings, from the *Mayflower Compact* to the Constitution itself."[3] Recognizing both importance of religion and the need to respect the inalienable right of religions liberty, the First Amendment prohibits government from enacting "an establishment of religion"[4] or "prohibiting the free exercise" of religion.[5] Although two Religion Clauses "often exert conflicting pressures,"[6] and there is frequently an "internal tension . . . between the Establishment Clause and the Free Exercise Clause,"[7] the Clauses "aim to foster a society in which people of all beliefs can live together harmoniously."[8] Like other provisions of the Bill of Rights, the Religion Clauses originally limited only the federal government and did not apply to state and local governments.[9] Thus, the States were free to do whatever they wished with respect to religion, subject only to the commands of their own State Constitutions. However, beginning in the 1940's, the Supreme Court held the Due Process Clause of the Fourteenth Amendment[10] incorporated both the Free Exercise[11] and the Establishment Clauses to state and local governments.[12]

This four-part chapter explores how the Religion Clauses affect public colleges and universities. Part I offers an overview of the Establishment Clause. Part II does the same for the Free Exercise Clause. Part III examines specific applications of the Religion Clauses on the campuses of public institutions of higher education. Part IV summarizes the major cases discussed in this chapter.

I. ESTABLISHMENT CLAUSE

The United States Constitution "does not say that in every and all aspects there shall be a separation of Church and State,"[13] but simply mandates "a freedom from laws instituting, supporting, or otherwise establishing religion."[14] The Establishment Clause also must be viewed "in the light of its history and the evils it was designed forever to suppress"[15] and must not be interpreted "with a literalness that would undermine the ultimate constitutional objective as illuminated by history."[16]

The Establishment Clause "does not prohibit practices which by any realistic measure create none of the dangers which it is designed to prevent and which do not so directly or substantially involve the state in religious exercises . . . as to have meaningful and practical impact."[17] This Clause permits "not only legitimate practices two centuries old but also any other practices with no greater potential for an establishment of religion."[18] Indeed, "there is nothing unconstitutional in a State's favoring religion generally, honoring God through public prayer and acknowledgment, or, in a non-proselytizing manner, venerating the Ten Commandments."[19]

"Government in our democracy, state and national, must be neutral in matters of religious theory, doctrine, and practice. It may not be hostile to any religion or to the advocacy of no religion; and it may not aid, foster, or promote one religion or religious theory against another or even against the militant opposite."[20] However, the Establishment Clause's mandate of neutrality is not absolute. Because a State is not required "to be oblivious to impositions that legitimate exercises of state power may place on religious belief and practice,"[21] it may extend benefits to religion that are not extended to nonreligion.[22] Similarly, while a State may not designate "a particular religious sect for special treatment,"[23] there is no requirement that a State's policies have the *same impact* on all religious sects.[24]

Since *Everson v. Board of Education* first applied the Establishment Clause to the States, the Supreme Court has addressed six distinct categories of cases.[25] First, "religious references or imagery in public monuments, symbols, mottos, displays, and ceremonies."[26] Second, "religious accommodations and exemptions from generally applicable laws."[27] Third, "subsidies and tax exemptions."[28] Fourth, "religious expression in public [K–12] schools."[29] Fifth, "regulation of private religious speech."[30] Sixth, "state interference with internal church affairs."[31] Of course, others do not fit into the categories,[32] such as cases concerning Sunday closing laws[33] and church involvement in governmental decision making.[34]

Given the wide variety of Establishment Clause cases, it is not surprising "there is no single formula for resolving Establishment Clause challenges.

Courts must instead consider each case in light of the basic purposes that the Religion Clauses were meant to serve."³⁵ Justice Kavanaugh has suggested Establishment Clause cases turn on "an overarching set of principles: If the challenged government practice is not coercive *and* if it (i) is rooted in history and tradition; or (ii) treats religious people, organizations, speech, or activity equally to comparable secular people, organizations, speech, or activity; or (iii) represents a permissible legislative accommodation or exemption from a generally applicable law."³⁶ Justice Kavanaugh's overarching set of principles explains existing Establishment Clause jurisprudence and may well represent a concise future approach to Establishment Clause issues.

Nevertheless, for the past fifty years, the Supreme Court has often, but not always, used the three-pronged test announced in *Lemon v. Kurtzman*.³⁷ Under the *Lemon* test, a court must ask whether a challenged government action (1) has a secular purpose; (2) has a "principal or primary effect" that "neither advances nor inhibits religion"; and (3) does not foster "an excessive government entanglement with religion."³⁸ When addressing the entanglement prong, a court must also examine "the character and purposes of the institutions that are benefitted, the nature of the aid that the State provides and the resulting relationship between the government and religious authority."³⁹ At least in the lower courts, *Lemon* has been the dominant mode of analysis.

Yet, as Justice Kavanaugh observed, "the *Lemon* test does not explain the Court's decisions in any of those . . . categories."⁴⁰ Justice Kavanaugh articulated six reasons for his belief.

First, "the Court has relied on history and tradition and upheld various religious symbols on government property and religious speech at government events. . . . *Lemon* does not account for the results in these cases."⁴¹ Second, the "Court has allowed legislative accommodations for religious activity and upheld legislatively granted religious exemptions from generally applicable laws. *Lemon*, fairly applied, does not justify those decisions."⁴² Third, "the Court likewise has upheld government benefits and tax exemptions that go to religious organizations, even though those policies have the effect of advancing or endorsing religion. Those outcomes are not easily reconciled with *Lemon*."⁴³

Fourth, "the Court has proscribed government-sponsored prayer in public schools. The Court has done so not because of *Lemon*, but because the Court concluded that government-sponsored prayer in public schools posed a risk of coercion of students. . . . In short, *Lemon* was not necessary to the Court's decisions holding government-sponsored school prayers unconstitutional.'⁴⁴ Fifth, the Court has allowed private religious speech in public forums on an equal basis with secular speech. . . *Lemon* does not explain those cases."⁴⁵ Sixth, the cases involving government interference with church affairs, such as *Hosanna-Tabor Evangelical Lutheran Church and School v. EEOC*, have never mentioned *Lemon*.[46]

Not surprisingly, "in many cases," the Supreme Court "has either expressly declined to apply the [*Lemon*] test or has simply ignored it."[47] As "cases involving a great array of laws and practices came to the Court, it became more and more apparent that the *Lemon* test could not resolve them."[48] Justice Thomas, in calling for the complete repudiation of *Lemon*, has argued: (1) it has no basis in the original meaning of the Constitution; (2) it is easily manipulated to achieve whatever result the judges wish; (3) it causes enormous confusion in both state and federal courts.[49] Justice Kavanaugh asserts the Court "no longer applies" *Lemon*.[50] Justice Gorsuch, joined by Justice Thomas, declared, "*Lemon* was a misadventure. It sought a 'grand unified theory' of the Establishment Clause but left us only a mess."[51] In short, if *Lemon* has relevance for Establishment Clause jurisprudence, it is diminished relevance.

While it is unclear how the Supreme Court will resolve future Establishment Clause cases, Justice Kavanaugh's overarching set of principles may provide a glimpse of the Court's future jurisprudence. As detailed above, Justice Kavanaugh essentially would ask: (1) whether the government policy is coercive; and (2) whether it is connected to historical practice or treats the sacred and secular similarly or creates an exemption from generally applicable laws for the free exercise of religion.[52]

II. FREE EXERCISE CLAUSE

While America had multiple beginnings,[53] the desire to worship God as the People saw fit was vital to the origin of Maryland, Rhode Island, and Utah.[54] The Free Exercise Clause of the First Amendment, which limits governments at all levels,[55] confirms this right.[56] Simply put, "the government, if it is to respect the Constitution's guarantee of free exercise, cannot impose regulations that are hostile to the religious beliefs of affected citizens and cannot act in a manner that passes judgment upon or presupposes the illegitimacy of religious beliefs and practices."[57] As Justice Gorsuch noted, "we know this with certainty: when the government fails to act neutrally toward the free exercise of religion, it tends to run into trouble."[58]

In addressing Free Exercise claims, the Supreme Court has consistently refused to "question the centrality of particular beliefs or practices to a faith, or the validity of particular litigants' interpretations of those creeds."[59] "Religious beliefs need not be acceptable, logical, consistent, or comprehensible to others in order to merit First Amendment protection."[60] The Court insists government "must not presume to determine the place of a particular belief in a religion or the plausibility of a religious claim."[61] To this end, "the First Amendment forbids civil [authorities] from" interpreting "particular church doctrines" and determining "the importance of those doctrines to the religion."[62] Moreover, "the guarantee of the Free Exercise Clause is not limited to beliefs which are shared by all of the members of a religious sect."[63] Public officials "have no business addressing whether the religious belief asserted" is reasonable.[64]

While the judiciary defers to the individual on what their faith requires, it is far less deferential when those religious beliefs require an individual to violate a neutral law of general applicability. The Supreme Court first articulated this principle in *Reynolds v. United States*, a dispute involving a ban on polygamy in the Utah territory.[65]

Since *Employment Division v. Smith* in 1990, "the right of free exercise does not relieve an individual of the obligation to comply with a 'valid and neutral law of general applicability on the ground that the law proscribes (or prescribes) conduct that his religion prescribes (or proscribes).'"[66] Under this standard, if a law is neutral and generally applicable, then there is no entitlement to a religious exemption.

Therefore, the key question is the meaning of neutrality and general applicability. Specifically, "a law that is neutral and of general applicability need not be justified by a compelling governmental interest even if the law has the incidental effect of burdening a particular religious practice."[67] Conversely, a law burdening religious practice that is neither neutral nor of general applicability must undergo the most rigorous of scrutiny.[68] "To satisfy the commands of the First Amendment, a law restrictive of religious practice must advance interests of the highest order and must be narrowly tailored in pursuit of those interests."[69] Although the two concepts are distinct, "neutrality and general applicability are interrelated, and failure to satisfy one requirement is a likely indication that the other has not been satisfied."[70]

"Government fails to act neutrally when it proceeds in a manner intolerant of religious beliefs or restricts practices because of their religious nature."[71] In other words, "a law is not neutral" if "the object of the law is to infringe upon or restrict practices because of their religious motivation."[72]

A law "lacks general applicability if it prohibits religious conduct while permitting secular conduct that undermines the government's asserted interests in a similar way."[73] "A law is not generally applicable if it 'invites' the government to consider the particular reasons for a person's conduct by providing 'a mechanism for individualized exemptions.'"[74] At the same time, government may not "impose burdens only conduct motivated by religious belief" in a "selective manner."[75] Furthermore, "the creation of a formal mechanism for granting exceptions renders a policy not generally applicable, regardless whether any exceptions have been given, because it invites the government to decide which reasons for not complying with the policy are worthy of solicitude."[76]

While the questions of neutrality and general applicability necessarily depend on the individual statute or policy at issue, the Court has articulated certain principles. "First, government regulations are not neutral and generally applicable . . . whenever they treat *any* comparable secular activity more favorably than religious exercise."[77] "Second, whether two activities are comparable for purposes of the Free Exercise Clause must be judged against the asserted government interest that justifies the regulation at issue."[78]

Conversely, if the statutes or policies at issue are *not* neutral and generally applicable, then the measures are constitutional "only if it advances 'interests of the highest order' and is narrowly tailored to achieve those interests."[79] "Put another way, so long as the government can achieve its interests in a manner that does not burden religion, it must do so."[80] "The government has the burden to establish that the challenged law satisfies strict scrutiny,"[81] but it cannot "rely on broadly formulated interests."[82] Instead, courts focus on "the asserted harm of granting specific exemptions to particular religious claimants."[83]

The holding in *Smith*, religious belief does not excuse compliance with a generally applicable neutral law, is controversial because of its departure from previous decisions. From 1963 to 1990, the Supreme Court ruled any governmental policy that substantially burdened the free exercise of religion was invalid unless the State could show a compelling governmental interest through the least restrictive means.[84] As a result, the Amish could refuse to send their older children to high school even though state law required attendance of children below the age of sixteen in school.[85]

Recognizing the effects of *Smith*, Congress and many States passed Religious Freedom Restoration Acts, which effectively restored the compelling governmental interest/least restrictive means standard.[86] More significantly, in 2021, five Justices expressed doubt about the validity of *Smith* while suggesting it should be overruled.[87]

III. APPLICATION OF THE RELIGION CLAUSES TO PUBLIC COLLEGES AND UNIVERSITIES

The Establishment Clause and the Free Exercise Clause, either separately or together, constrain officials at public colleges and universities in four ways. First, although the Establishment Clause applies to public universities just as it applies to all constitutional actors, concerns about establishment are diminished in higher education because the students are adults rather than children. Second, if college and university officials extend programs or benefits for secular individuals or organizations, then they must allow religious persons or religious organizations to participate in the program or receive the benefit.

Third, while *Christian Legal Society v. Martinez* has not been overruled, recent Supreme Court decisions suggest student religious organizations have the right to exclude those who disagree with the tenets of the faith. If so, then campus officials cannot interfere with the religious group's organizational autonomy. Fourth, to the extent that college and university officials grant exemptions from a particular policy, they must grant religious exemptions to religious individuals and religious organizations. Each of these applications is discussed in some detail below.

A. Establishment Clause Concerns Are Diminished in Higher Education

The Establishment Clause applies to public colleges and universities, but concerns about establishment are diminished in higher education.

To explain, in *Lee v. Weisman*, the Supreme Court held it was unconstitutional for the principal of a public middle school to invite a local religious leader to offer prayers in the form of an invocation and benediction at middle school graduation ceremony.[88] In doing so, the Court expressed its fear that the prayers were psychologically coercive to the graduating children because, as captive audience, they may have been forced against their wills to be part of a ceremony from which they were not genuinely free to be excused.[89] While the Court relied on psychological coercion in *Lee*, it ignored this concept in *Santa Fe Independent School District v. Doe*, where it reached a similar result concerning prayer before a high school football game.[90]

While the Court was concerned about forcing children to miss the graduation ceremony or hear the prayer in *Lee*, the Court explicitly declined to "address whether that choice is acceptable if the affected citizens are mature adults, but we think the State may not . . . place primary and secondary school children in this position."[91] As the Court remarked, "there are heightened concerns with protecting freedom of conscience from subtle coercive pressure in the elementary and secondary public schools."[92]

In deciding Establishment Clause cases, "the Supreme Court has always considered the age of the audience an important factor in the [Establishment Clause] analysis."[93] As the Court noted in *Widmar v. Vincent*, "University students are, of course, young adults. They are less impressionable than younger students and should be able to appreciate that the University's policy is one of neutrality toward religion."[94] This distinction between children and adults prompted the Sixth and Seventh Circuits to uphold prayer at graduation ceremonies,[95] but did not prevent the Fourth Circuit from invalidating prayer at a state military academy's evening meal.[96]

B. When Officials at Public Colleges and Universities Create Programs, the Officials Cannot Exclude Religious Organizations and Individuals

Officials at public colleges and universities often create programs benefiting organizations or individuals, but sometimes refuse to allow religious organizations or people of faith to take part in these programs. For example, officials often refuse to fund activities of student religious groups that, in their judgments, are "worship activities" or proselytizing while expressly permitting funding for virtually identical activities by secular groups.[97]

Administrators might allow the leaders of the French Club to buy bread and wine for its functions, but deny the officers of the Roman Catholic Club's request to buy bread and wine. The administrators might subsidize the community outreach activities of political groups or advocacy groups, but refuse to support the evangelism activities of religious groups.[98] Institutional officials often justify these exclusions by claiming that allowing religious organizations or persons to participate would violate the Establishment Clause. In some instances, administrators rely on state law provisions prohibiting actions that are permissible under the Establishment Clause.

Two recent Supreme Court cases, *Trinity Lutheran Church v. Comer*[99] and *Espinoza v. Montana Department of Taxation*,[100] hold government may not exclude religious organizations and religious individuals from participation in governmental programs solely because the organizations are religious.[101] For instance, there is no obligation for the States to fund private K-12 education, but, if the States chooses to subsidize private education, the States cannot exclude religious schools solely because they are religious.[102] To be sure, there is "some space" for policy choices "neither compelled by the Free Exercise Clause nor prohibited by the Establishment Clause,"[103] but the judgments in *Trinity Lutheran* and *Espinoza* narrowed that space.[104]

Trinity Lutheran and *Espinoza* represent a reaffirmation of the long-standing rule in higher education. In Both *Widmar* and *Rosenberger v. Rector & Visitors of the University of Virginia*, discussed in Chapter 1, the Supreme Court determined student religious organizations must receive recognition, access, or funding on the same terms as secular student organizations. As those cases made clear, the Establishment Clause does not require the exclusion of student religious organizations while the First Amendment Free Speech Clause requires their inclusion.[105]

C. Public Institutional Administrators May Not Interfere with the Institutional Autonomy of a Religious Organization

As highlighted in Chapter 1 on the Freedom of Speech, in *Christian Legal Society*, the Supreme Court declared officials of public colleges and universities could, through an "all comers" policies, require a student group to admit any student, including students who disagreed with the group's organizational values and objectives. Consequently, a student religious group could be forced to accept members who emphatically reject key tenets of the faith. Conversely, at some institutions, secular student groups are allowed to exclude those who disagree with their views, but the religious organizations are required to refrain from what critics describe as religious discrimination as they seek to preserve their faith-based identities and organizational autonomy.[106] In applying this policy, it is unclear why the Young Democrats may have excluded Republicans, but Evangelical Christian Clubs could not have denied membership to atheists.[107]

Like all Supreme Court decisions, *Christian Legal Society* remains binding precedent until overruled,[108] but two recent Supreme Court cases establish a principle of autonomy for religious organizations that seems incompatible with *Christian Legal Society*.

First, in *Hosanna-Tabor Evangelical Lutheran Church & School v. EEOC*,[109] the Supreme Court unanimously concluded that "[b]oth Religion Clauses bar the government from interfering with the decision of a religious group to fire one of its ministers."[110] Emphasizing both the right of "hierarchical religious organizations to establish their own rules and regulations for internal discipline and government, and to create tribunals for adjudicating disputes over these matters,"[111] the Court declared, "there is such a ministerial exception."[112] "The members of a religious group put their faith in the hands of their ministers. Requiring a church to accept or retain an unwanted minister, or punishing a church for failing to do so, intrudes upon more than a mere employment decision."[113]

In reaching this outcome, the Supreme Court emphasized the First Amendment "gives special solicitude to the rights of religious organizations. We cannot accept the remarkable view that the Religion Clauses have nothing to say about a religious organization's freedom to select its own [leaders]."[114] "By imposing an unwanted minister, the state infringes the Free Exercise Clause, which protects a religious group's right to shape its own faith and mission through its appointments."[115] "According the state the power to determine which individuals will minister to the faithful also violates the Establishment Clause, which prohibits government involvement in such ecclesiastical decisions."[116]

Second, in *Our Lady of Guadalupe v. Morrisey-Berru*,[117] the Supreme Court expanded the scope of the Religion Clauses' "ministerial exception," to include teachers in Roman Catholic schools who were not ordained ministers, had no religious training, and who taught secular subjects.[118] In its analysis, the Court noted that a "variety of factors may be important" in determining if the ministerial exception applies.[119]

In *Our Lady,* the Supreme Court held government officials must acknowledge a religious organization's "autonomy with respect to internal management decisions that are essential to the institution's central mission. And a component of this autonomy is the selection of the individuals who play certain key roles."[120] "When a school with a religious mission entrusts a teacher with the responsibility of educating and forming students in the faith," the First Amendment prohibits "judicial intervention into disputes between the school and the teacher."[121] While the Court gave significant deference to the leaders of the religious organization's judgment, Justice Thomas, joined by Justice Gorsuch, would give absolute deference: "The Religion Clauses require civil courts to defer to religious organizations' good-faith claims that a certain employee's position is 'ministerial.'"[122]

Together, *Hosanna-Tabor* and *Our Lady of Guadalupe* establish the principle that leaders of religious organizations, including student religious groups, have a right of absolute discretion to determine who their leaders will be. Logically, if officials in religious organizations can restrict their leadership to those who adhere to the faith and basic principles, then the leaders ought to be able to apply a similar standard to those individuals seeking membership. The necessary inference of *Hosanna-Tabor* and our *Lady of Guadalupe* is that student religious organizations, through the Religion Clauses, have greater associational freedoms than their secular counterparts. Because the government may favor religion and religious entities over nonreligion and nonreligious entities, such a result would not violate the Establishment Clause.[123]

D. If Officials at Public Colleges and Universities Grant Exemptions from Policies, the Officials Must Grant Religious Exemptions

Officials at public colleges and universities frequently have policies or rules that are applicable to everyone but also have a mechanism for exemptions from the policies. To illustrate, institutional policies may require employees and students to be vaccinated, but individuals with specific medical conditions may obtain an exemption. Similarly, faculty members may require students to attend every class, but may grant exemptions for genuine illnesses or when students are representing the institution in some other activities.

If institutional officials grant any exemptions for any reason, there must be a mechanism in place for religious exemptions. "The creation of a formal mechanism for granting exceptions renders a policy not generally applicable, regardless of whether any exceptions have been given, because it invites the government to decide which reasons for not complying with the policy are worthy of solicitude."[124] In other words, if medical exemptions are available from vaccination requirements, then there must be religious exemptions. Similarly, if students are exempt from attendance for any reason, there must be a mechanism for students to have excused absences for religious purposes.

In assessing an application for a religious exemption, officials at public colleges and universities should not "question the centrality of particular beliefs or practices to a faith, or the validity of particular litigants' interpretations of those creeds."[125] "Religious beliefs need not be acceptable, logical, consistent, or comprehensible to others in order to merit First Amendment protection."[126] As such, college and university officials should assume the applicant is sincere in their faith.[127]

Of course, there are likely to be circumstances when college and university officials do not offer an exemption, but compliance requires an individual to violate their faith. As discussed in Chapter 1 on the Freedom of Speech, some professional groups, such as psychological counselors or social workers, impose ethical requirements on those who are part of those professions.[128] Yet, adhering to those ethical standards requirements may require People of Faith to violate their religious beliefs.[129] As part of preparing students to enter these professions, faculty members at public colleges and universities may insist students conform to the profession's ethics and ignore their faith convictions.[130]

When confronted with a claim for religious exemptions, the lower federal appellate courts have agreed that religious students must conform to the ethics of their intended professions,[131] but have insisted that students with religious objections be treated the same as those students who are secular.[132] Nevertheless, the insistence that religious students conform to professional ethics that are antithetical to their beliefs can chill such individuals from even entering these professions.[133]

IV. SUMMARY OF THE MAJOR CASES DISCUSSED IN THIS CHAPTER

American Legion v. American Humanist Association, 139 S. Ct. 2067 (2019)

The Supreme Court interpreted the Establishment Clause using an analysis that emphasized historical context. As a result, the Court allowed a memorial cross commemorating the death of soldiers in World War I to remain on a public highway in Maryland as not violating the Establishment Clause because with the passage of time it took on a secular message linked to those who died in battle rather than advancing Christianity.

Christian Legal Society v. Martinez, 561 U.S. 661 (2010)

Because the Supreme Court held a public university may require recognized student organizations to admit "all comers" as a condition of recognition, a student religious group was required to admit students who disagreed with its beliefs.

Church of the Lukumi Babalu Aye v. City of Hialeah, 508 U.S. 520 (1993)

The Supreme Court decided a law lacks facial neutrality for purposes of the Free Exercise Clause if it refers to a religious practice without a secular meaning discernible from the language or context. As a result, the Court found a local government violated the Free Exercise Clause.

Employment Division, Department of Human Resources of Oregon v. Smith, 494 U.S. 872 (1990)

The Supreme Court modified the standard for determining if there was a violation of the Free Exercise Clause. If there is a religiously neutral statute of general applicability, there is no requirement for government to grant a religious exemption. Consequently, the Court upheld the dismissal of drug counselors who ingested peyote as part of a sacramental ritual in the Native American Church. The decision prompted Congress to pass the Religious Freedom Restoration Act. Several States have enacted similar laws.

Espinoza v. Montana Department of Taxation, 140 S. Ct. 2246 (2020)

The Supreme Court ruled that a State could not adopt a state constitutional provision which created greater separation between church and state than required by the National Constitution.

Fulton v. City of Philadelphia, Pennsylvania, 141 S. Ct. 1868 (2021)

The Supreme Court decided when government has a mechanism for granting secular exemptions but not religious exemptions, the policy is not neutral and generally applicable. Accordingly, the Court enjoined the enforcement of a policy that burdened a religious agency's First Amendment right to the free exercise of religion by having to curtail its mission of providing foster care for children or approving relationships inconsistent with its beliefs.

Hosanna-Tabor Evangelical Lutheran Church and School v. EEOC, 565 U.S. 171 (2012)

The Supreme Court determined the First Amendment Religious Clause contained a ministerial exception, which guarantees a large degree of autonomy to religious organizations. As a result, rejecting the age discrimination claim of a teacher in a faith-based school could not pursue an age discrimination claim.

Our Lady of Guadalupe v. Morrisey-Berru, 140 S. Ct. 2049 (2020)

The Supreme Court held the ministerial exception, grounded in the First Amendment, barred private school teachers in California from filing employment discrimination claims against their religious schools. The case is significant for expanding the autonomy rights of religious organizations.

Rosenberger v. Rector and Visitors of University of Virginia, 515 U.S. 819 (1995)

The Supreme Court ruled if university officials decided to fund student publication, then the officials could not deny funding to a Christian publication. The case is significant both for preventing viewpoint discrimination and finding funding of a religious message does not violate the Establishment Clause.

Trinity Lutheran Church v. Comer, 137 S. Ct. 2012 (2017)

The Supreme Court decided the Establishment Clause does not allow Missouri or other states to single out faith-based institutions, and/or believers, to deny generally available benefits simply because they are religious.

Widmar v. Vincent, 454 U.S. 263 (1981)

The Supreme Court held that when officials at a state university made facilities generally available for activities of registered student groups, they could not prevent faith-based organizations from gathering due to the religious content of their speech.

NOTES

1. *Roman Catholic Diocese of Brooklyn v. Cuomo*, 141 S. Ct. 63, 70 (2020) (Gorsuch, J., concurring).
2. *Zorach v. Clauson*, 343 U.S. 306, 313 (1952).
3. *School District of Abington Township. v. Schempp*, 374 U.S. 203, 213 (1963).
4. U.S. Const. amend I (Establishment Clause).
5. U.S. Const. amend. I (Free Exercise Clause).
6. *Cutter v. Wilkinson*, 544 U.S. 709, 719 (2005).
7. *Tilton v. Richardson*, 403 U.S. 672, 677 (1971) (plurality opinion).
8. *American Legion v. American Humanist Association*, 139 S. Ct. 2067, 2074 (2019).
9. See *Barron v. Mayor and City Council of Baltimore*, 32 U.S. (7 Pet.) 243, 249 (1833).
10. U.S. Const. amend. XIV, § 1. (Due Process Clause).
11. *Cantwell v. Connecticut*, 310 U.S. 296, 303 (1940).
12. *Everson v. Board of Education*, 330 U.S. 1, 17–18 (1947).
13. *Zorach*, 343 U.S. at 312.
14. Phillip Hamburger, Separation of Church and State 2 (2003).
15. *Everson*, 330 U.S. at 14–15.
16. *Walz v. Tax Commission*, 397 U.S. 664, 671 (1970).
17. *Schempp*, 374 U.S. at 308 (Goldberg, J., joined by Harlan, J. concurring).
18. *County of Allegheny v. ACLU*, 492 U.S. 573, 670 (1989). (Kennedy, J., joined by Rehnquist, C.J., White & Scalia, JJ., concurring).
19. *Van Orden v. Perry* 545 U.S. 677, 692 (2005) (Scalia, J., concurring).
20. *Epperson v. Arkansas*, 393 U.S. 97, 103–4 (1968).
21. *Board of Education of Kiryas Joel Village School District v. Grumet*, 512 U.S. 687, 705 (1994).
22. *Cutter*, 544 U.S. at 720.
23. *Grumet*, 512 U.S. at 706–7.

24. *Gillette v. United States,* 401 U.S. 437, 454 (1971).

25. *American Legion v. American Humanist Association,* 139 S. Ct 2067, 2082 n. 16 (2019).

26. *Id. See, e.g., Lynch v. Donnelly,* 465 U.S. 668 (1984); *Van Orden,* 545 U.S. at 677.

27. *American Legion,* 139 S. Ct. at 2082 n. 16. *See e.g., Cutter v. Wilkinson,* 544 U.S. 709 (2005); *Corporation of Presiding Bishop of Church of Jesus Christ of Latter-day Saints v. Amos,* 483 U.S. 327 (1987).

28. *American Legion,* 139 S. Ct. at 2082 n. 16. *See, e.g., Walz v. Tax Commission of City of New York,* 397 U.S. 664 (1970); *Zelman v. Simmons-Harris,* 536 U.S. 639 (2002).

29. *American Legion,* 139 S. Ct. at 2082 n. 16. *See, e.g., School District of Abington Township v. Schempp,* 374 U.S. 203 (1963); *Lee v. Weisman,* 505 U.S. 577 (1992).

30. *American Legion,* 139 S. Ct. at 2082 n. 16. *See, e.g., Capitol Square Review and Advisory Board v. Pinette,* 515 U.S. 753 (1995).

31. *American Legion,* 139 S. Ct. at 2082 n. 16. *See, e.g., Hosanna-Tabor Evangelical Lutheran Church and School v. EEOC,* 565 U.S. 171 (2012).

32. *American Legion,* 139 S. Ct. at 2082 n. 16.

33. *McGowan v. Maryland,* 366 U.S. 420 (1961).

34. *See, e.g., Larkin v. Grendel's Den, Inc.,* 459 U.S. 116 (1982); *Board of Education of Kiryas Joel Village School District v. Grumet,* 512 U.S. 687 (1994).

35. *American Legion,* 139 S. Ct. at 2090–91 (2019) (Breyer, J., joined by Kagan, J., concurring).

36. *Id.* at 2093 (Kavanaugh, J., concurring).

37. *Lemon v. Kurtzman,* 403 U. S. 602 (1971).

38. *Id.* at 612–13.

39. *Id.* at 615.

40. *American Legion,* 139 S. Ct. at 2092 (Kavanaugh, J., concurring).

41. *Id.*

42. *Id.*

43. *Id.* at 2092–93 (Kavanaugh, J., concurring).

44. *Id.*

45. *Id.*

46. *Hosanna-Tabor Evangelical Lutheran Church and School v. EEOC.* 565 U.S. 171 (2012).

47. *American Legion,* 139 S. Ct. at 2080.

48. *Id.*

49. *Id.* at 2097–98 (Thomas, J., concurring).

50. *Id.* at 2092 (Kavanaugh, J., concurring).

51. *Id.* at 2101 (Gorsuch, J., joined by Kavanaugh, J., concurring).

52. *Id.* at 2093 (Kavanaugh, J., concurring).

53. *See* Colin Woodard, AMERICAN NATIONS: A HISTORY OF THE ELEVEN REGIONAL CULTURES OF NORTH AMERICA (2011).

54. *See* Jeffery Sutton, 51 IMPERFECT SOLUTIONS: STATES AND THE MAKING OF AMERICAN CONSTITUTIONAL LAW 17 (2018).

55. *Cantwell*, 310 U.S. at 303.

56. U.S. Const. amend. I (Free Exercise Clause).

57. *Masterpiece Cakeshop v. Colorado Civil Rights Commission*, 138 S. Ct. 1719, 1731 (2018).

58. *Id.* at 1734 (Gorsuch, J. concurring).

59. *Employment Division, Department of Human Resources of Oregon v. Smith*, 494 U.S. 872, 887 (1990).

60. *Fulton v. City of Philadelphia*, 141 S. Ct. 1868, 1876 (2021).

61. *Smith*, 494 U.S. at 887.

62. *Presbyterian Church in United States v. Mary Elizabeth Blue Hull Memorial Presbyterian Church*, 393 U.S. 440, 450 (1969).

63. *Holt v. Hobbs*, 574 U.S. 352, 362 (2015).

64. *Burwell v. Hobby Lobby Stores, Inc.*, 573 U.S. 682, 724 (2014).

65. *Reynolds v. United States*, 98 U.S. 145 (1878).

66. *Smith*, 494 U.S. at 879.

67. *Church of the Lukumi Babalu Aye, Inc v. City of Hialeah*, 508 U.S. 520, 531 (1993).

68. *Id.* at 546.

69. *Id.*

70. *Id.* at 531.

71. *Fulton*, 141 S. Ct. at 1877.

72. *Lukumi*, 508 U.S. at 533.

73. *Fulton*, 141 S. Ct. at 1877.

74. *Id.*

75. *Lukumi*, 508 U.S. at 543.

76. *Fulton*, 141 S. Ct. at 1877.

77. *Tandon v. Newsom*, 141 S. Ct. 1294, 1296 (2021).

78. *Id.*

79. *Fulton*, 141 S. Ct. at 1881.

80. *Id.*

81. *Tandon*, 141 S. Ct. at 1296.

82. *Fulton*, 141 S. Ct. at 1881.

83. *Id.*

84. *Sherbert v. Verner*, 374 U.S. 398, 402–3 (1963).

85. *Wisconsin v. Yoder*, 406 U.S. 205, 214–15 (1972).

86. 42 U.S.C. § 2000bb et seq.; Ala. Const. art. I, § 3.01; Ariz. Rev. Stat. § 41–1493.01; Ark Code 16–123–401; Conn. Gen. Stat. § 52–571b; Fla. Stat. § 767.01; Idaho Code § 73–402; Ill. Rev. Stat. Ch. 775, § 35/1; Ind. Code 34–13–9–5; Kan. Stat. §60–5301, et seq.; Ky. Rev. Stat. §446.350; La. Rev. Stat. §13:5231, et seq.; Miss. Code §11–61–1 Mo. Rev. Stat. §1.302; N.M. Stat. §28–22–1, et seq; Okla. Stat. tit. 51, §251, et seq. Pa. Stat. tit. 71, §2403; R.I. Gen. Laws §42–80.1-1, et seq., S.C. Code §1–32–10, et seq.; Tenn. Code §4–1–407; Tex. Civ. Prac. & Remedies Code §110.001, et seq; Va. Code §57–1, et seq.

87. *Fulton*, 141 S. Ct. at 1882–83 (Barrett, J., joined by Kavanaugh, J., concurring); *Id.* at 1888–89 (Alito, J., joined by Thomas & Gorsuch, J., concurring).

88. *Lee v. Wiseman*, 505 U.S. 577 (1990).
89. *Id.*
90. *Santa Fe Independent School District v. Doe*, 530 U.S. 290 (2000).
91. *Lee*, 505 U.S. at 593.
92. *Id.* at 592.
93. *Chaudhuri v. Tennessee.*, 130 F.3d 232, 239 (6th Cir. 1997).
94. *Widmar v. Vincent*, 454 U.S. 263, 274 n. 14 (1981).
95. *Chaudhuri*, 130 F.3d at 239; *Tanford v. Brand*, 104 F.3d 982 (7th Cir. 1997).
96. *Mellen v. Bunting*, 327 F.3d 355, 371–72 (4th Cir. 2003).
97. *See Roman Catholic Foundation, UW-Madison, Inc. v. Regents of University of Wisconsin System*, 578 F. Supp. 2d 1121, 1134–36 (W.D. Wis. 2008), *aff'd sub nom. Badger Catholic, Inc. v. Walsh*, 620 F.3d 775 (7th Cir. 2010).
98. *Roman Catholic Foundation*, 578 F. Supp. 2d at 1134–36.
99. *Trinity Lutheran Church v. Comer*, 137 S. Ct. 2012 (2017).
100. *Espinoza v. Montana Department of Taxation*, 140 S. Ct. 2246 (2020).
101. *Id.* at 2256.
102. *Id.* at 2261.
103. *Cutter*, 544 U.S. at 719.
104. *Espinoza*, 140 S. Ct. at 2260–61.
105. *Rosenberger v. Rector and Visitors of University of Virginia*, 515 U.S. 819, 838–46 (1995). *Widmar*, 454 U.S. at 271–75.
106. *Alpha Delta Chi-Delta Chapter v. Reed*, 648 F.3d 790 (9th Cir. 2011).
107. *Id.* at 800–801.
108. *Agostini v. Felton*, 521 U.S. 203, 237–38 (1997).
109. *Hosanna-Tabor Evangelical Lutheran Church and School v. EEOC*, 565 U.S. 171 (2012).
110. *Id.* at 182–83.
111. *Serbian Eastern Orthodox Diocese for United States and Canada v. Milivojevich*, 426 U.S. 696, 724 (1976).
112. *Hosanna Tabor*, 565 U.S. at 188.
113. *Id.*
114. *Id.* at 189.
115. *Id.* at 188.
116. *Id.* at 188–89.
117. *Our Lady of Guadalupe v. Morrisey-Berru*, 140 S. Ct. 2049 (2020).
118. *Id.* at 2055.
119. *Id.* at 2063.
120. *Id.* at 2060.
121. *Id.* at 2069.
122. *Id.* at 2069–70 (Thomas, J., joined by Gorsuch, concurring).
123. *See Cutter*, 544 U.S. at 719–24; *Texas Monthly, Inc. v. Bullock*, 489 U.S. 1, 18 n.8 (1989); *Corporations. of the Presiding Bishop of the Church of Jesus Christ of Latter-Day Saints v. Amos*, 483 U.S. 327, 335 (1987).
124. *Fulton*, 141 S. Ct. at 1879.
125. *Hernandez v. Commissioner of Internal Revenue*, 490 U.S. 680, 699 (1989).

126. *Thomas v. Review Board*, 450 U.S. 707, 714 (1981).
127. *Resurrection School v. Hertel*, 11 F.4th 437, 455 (6th Cir. 2021).
128. Todd A. DeMitchell, David T. Herbert, & Loan T. Phan, *The University Curriculum and the Constitution: Personal Beliefs and Professional Ethics in Graduate School Counseling Programs*, 39 J.C. & U.L. 303, 304–5 (2013).
129. Douglas Laycock, *Religious Liberty and the Culture Wars*, 2014 U. ILL. L. REV. 839, 872–73 (2014) (footnotes omitted).
130. DeMitchell, Herbert, & Phan, *supra* note 128, at 305.
131. *Keeton v. Anderson-Wiley*, 664 F.3d 865, 874 (11th Cir. 2011).
132. *Ward v. Polite*, 667 F.3d 727, 735-38 (6th Cir. 2012).
133. Laycock, *supra* note 129, at 872–73.

Chapter 3

Neither Knows nor Tolerates Classes

Equal Protection

> The Constitution neither knows nor tolerates classes among its citizens.—
> *Romer v. Evans*[1]

The Equal Protection Clause,[2] is "essentially a direction that all persons similarly situated . . . be treated alike,"[3] and that the Constitution protects "*persons*, not *groups*."[4] Indeed, the "rights created by the first section of the Fourteenth Amendment are, by its terms, guaranteed to the individual. The rights established are personal rights."[5] As Justice Douglas wrote, "here the individual is important, not his race, his creed, or his color."[6] "The guarantee of equal protection cannot mean one thing when applied to one individual and something else when applied to a person of another color. If both are not accorded the same protection, then it is not equal."[7] Conversely, if the government treats everyone equally, there is no equal protection violation.[8]

Despite the absolute nature of the constitutional text, the Equal Protection Clause does not prohibit all governmental classifications.[9] "Most laws classify, and many affect certain groups unevenly, even though the law itself treats them no differently from all other members of the class described by the law. When the basic classification is rationally based, uneven effects upon particular groups within a class are ordinarily of no constitutional concern."[10] The "general rule is that legislation is presumed to be valid and will be sustained if the classification drawn by the statute is rationally related to a legitimate state interest."[11] This general rule gives way in those rare instances when statutes infringe upon fundamental constitutional rights or use "suspect" or "quasi-suspect" classifications.[12]

Courts "apply different levels of scrutiny to different types of classifications."[13] "Classifications based on race or national origin . . . and classifications affecting fundamental rights . . . are given the most exacting scrutiny."[14] Some classifications are subjected to "intermediate scrutiny, which generally has been applied to discriminatory classifications based on sex or illegitimacy."[15] All other classifications are subjected to "rational basis" review, which requires that "a statutory classification must be rationally related to a legitimate governmental purpose."[16]

This seven-part chapter discusses how the Equal Protection applies in different contexts on a public campus. Part I deals with race. Part II covers sex. Part III addresses sexual orientation and gender identity. Part IV examines alienage. Part V discusses disability. Part VI reviews other classification. Part VII summarizes the major cases discussed in this Chapter.

I. RACE

Governmental policies that classify people by race are presumptively invalid.[17]

"One of the principal reasons race is treated as a forbidden classification is that it demeans the dignity and worth of a person to be judged by ancestry instead of by his or her own merit and essential qualities."[18] Indeed, racial distinctions "are by their very nature odious to a free people whose institutions are founded upon the doctrine of equality"[19] and are "contrary to our traditions and hence constitutionally suspect."[20] The right of individuals "to be treated with equal dignity and respect are implicated by a rigid rule erecting race as the sole criterion in an aspect of public decision-making."[21] As Justice Brennan observed, "an explicit policy of assignment by race may serve to stimulate our society's latent race-consciousness."[22] "Absent searching judicial inquiry into the justification for such race-based measures, we have no way to determine what classifications are 'benign' or 'remedial' and what classifications are in fact motivated by illegitimate notions of racial inferiority or simple racial politics.'"[23] Consequently, the Constitution imposes two special rules for any racial classification.

First, "all racial classifications, imposed by whatever federal, state, or local governmental actor, must be analyzed by a reviewing court under strict scrutiny."[24] Recognizing that "racial characteristics so seldom provide a relevant basis for disparate treatment,"[25] racial classifications "are constitutional only if they are narrowly tailored to further compelling governmental interests."[26] This is a very demanding standard, which few programs can survive.[27] As Chief Justice Roberts, joined by Justices Scalia, Thomas, and Alito, observed, "the way to stop discrimination on the basis of race is to stop discrimination on the basis of race."[28]

At the same time, the fact government might use racial classifications to *help* racial minorities does not change the analysis. "[T]he analysis and level of scrutiny applied to determine the validity of [a racial] classification do not vary simply because the objective appears acceptable. . . . While the validity and importance of the objective may affect the outcome of the analysis, the analysis itself does not change."[29]

As the Supreme Court declared, "the mere recitation of a 'benign' or legitimate purpose for a racial classification is entitled to little or no weight. Racial classifications are suspect, and that means that simple legislative assurances of good intention cannot suffice."[30] "Despite the surface appeal of holding 'benign' racial classifications to a lower standard, because 'it may not always be clear that a so-called preference is in fact benign.'"[31] Therefore, the Court has "insisted on strict scrutiny in every context, even for so-called 'benign' racial classifications, such as race-conscious university admissions or hiring policies, race-based preferences in government contracts, and race-based districting intended to improve minority representation."[32]

As Justice Thomas explained, the fact "these programs may be motivated, in part, by good intentions cannot provide refuge from the principle that under our Constitution, the government may not make distinctions on the basis of race."[33] From a constitutional standpoint, "it is irrelevant whether a government's racial classifications are drawn by those who wish to oppress a race or by those who have a sincere desire to help those thought to be disadvantaged."[34] In other words, "the paternalism that appears to lie at the heart of this program is at war with the principle of inherent equality that underlies and infuses our Constitution."[35]

Second, when dealing with racial classifications, the presumptions of constitutionality and burden of proof are flipped. Instead of presuming that governmental action is constitutional[36] and requiring the challenger to demonstrate otherwise,[37] "the government has the burden of proving that racial classifications 'are narrowly tailored measures that further compelling governmental interests.'"[38]

The remainder of this part of the chapter addresses the potential compelling governmental interests and the requirements of narrow tailoring.

A. Compelling Governmental Interests

For public institutions of higher education, the Supreme Court has recognized only two goals as constitutionally sufficient justification for race-conscious decision-making. First, in the context of higher education admissions, the Court held obtaining the educational benefits of a diverse student body is a compelling governmental interest.[39] While this compelling interest in admissions likely extends to higher education scholarship, neither the Supreme Court nor any lower court has extended it to faculty or administrative hiring.

Second, in all contexts, the Supreme Court has held there is a compelling governmental interest in remedying the present-day effects of past intentional discrimination by a governmental entity such as the public college or university.[40] As discussed in more detail below, past discrimination is not enough to justify race-based decision-making. Rather, there must still be present-day effects of that discrimination. For example, the fact a university did not admit African Americans until the 1970's does not necessarily mean there are present day effects of that discrimination in the 2020's. Similarly, the fact one university engaged in intentional discrimination and there are lingering effects of this unconstitutional conduct does not justify the use of race by another institution.

Just as significantly, the Supreme Court has explicitly rejected many other proposed compelling governmental interests. The Court has repeatedly ruled[41] "remedying past societal discrimination does not justify race-conscious government action."[42] The Court has also rejected maintaining racial balance,[43] correcting underrepresentation of minorities,[44] providing faculty role models for students,[45] increasing the number of physicians in underserved areas, in a profession,[46] and making "the objective of supplier diversity a reality."[47]

Yet, each of the two compelling governmental interests—remedying the present-day effects of past intentional discrimination by the public institution itself and obtaining the educational benefits of a diverse student body—is difficult for officials at public institutions to achieve. Accordingly, this subpart examines both issues.

1. Obtaining the Educational Benefits of a Diverse Student Body

In academe, racial and ethnic diversity is sacrosanct. Institutional officials desperately want to increase the number of students and faculty members from specific racial minorities. To do so, officials believe it is necessary to have some consideration of race in the decision-making process. Yet, because most public colleges and universities do not have a history of past intentional discrimination or have eliminated the present-day effects of that discrimination, institutional officials must focus on obtaining the educational benefits of a diverse student body.

Contrary to the beliefs of many in higher education, the Supreme Court has never held "an interest in simple ethnic diversity, in which a specified percentage of the student body is in effect guaranteed to be members of selected ethnic groups, with the remaining percentage an undifferentiated aggregation of students" is a compelling governmental interest.[48] "A university is not permitted to define diversity as 'some specified percentage of a particular group merely because of its race or ethnic origin.'"[49] "That would amount to outright racial balancing, which is patently unconstitutional."[50] "Racial balancing is not transformed from 'patently unconstitutional' to a compelling state interest simply by relabeling it 'racial diversity.'"[51]

Rather, the Supreme Court has found that officials at state institutions of higher education have "a compelling interest in obtaining the *educational benefits* that flow from a diverse student body."[52] In doing so, the Court explicitly embraced the concept of diversity articulated by Justice Powell in 1978.[53] In Justice Powell's view, "the diversity that furthers a compelling state interest encompasses a far broader array of qualifications and characteristics of which racial or ethnic origin is but a single though important element."[54]

The Supreme Court's rationale for allowing the consideration of race is not remedying societal discrimination; it is to ensure increased "exposure to widely diverse people, cultures, ideas, and viewpoints."[55] "[T]he classroom is peculiarly the 'marketplace of ideas.' The Nation's future depends upon leaders trained through wide exposure to that robust exchange of ideas which discovers truth 'out of a multitude of tongues, (rather) than through any kind of authoritative selection.'"[56] "The atmosphere of 'speculation, experiment and creation'—so essential to the quality of higher education—is widely believed to be promoted by a diverse student body."[57] Put another way, the Supreme Court's rationale for pursuing racial and ethnic diversity is the free speech ideal.[58]

The link between the educational benefits of a diverse student body and the free speech ideal implicitly imposes other obligations on officials at public colleges or universities. It is not enough to admit students because of their unique experiences, attitudes, and beliefs; the administrators must encourage students to engage in dialogue.[59] Nor is it enough to welcome underrepresented populations to campus; the students must recognize "free speech must be the rule for any truly pluralistic or multicultural community. Far from requiring censorship, a true understanding of multiculturalism demands free speech."[60] Indeed, when the expression of *any* demographic, religious, or political minority is limited, the majority suffers because it is not exposed to the viewpoints of the minority groups.

2. Remedying the Present-Day Effects of Past Intentional Discrimination by the Public College or University

Outside of the admissions or scholarship context, the only compelling governmental interest that could justify the use of race is remedying the present-day effects of past intentional discrimination by the university. If officials at public colleges or universities wish to engage in race-based decision-making with respect to hiring or procurement, then they will need to justify the use of race with remedying the present-day effects of past intentional discrimination by their institution.

If the government asserts there are present day effects of past intentional discrimination, there must be specific findings[61] of actual present-day effects of such past discrimination.[62] "Proper findings in this regard are necessary to define both the scope of the injury and the extent of the remedy necessary to cure its effects."[63] "Findings also serve to assure all citizens that the deviation from the norm of equal treatment of all racial and ethnic groups is a temporary matter, a measure taken in the service of the goal of equality itself."[64] In assessing the government's findings, four considerations are relevant.

First, while the findings of legislative bodies are generally entitled to great deference,[65] a racial classification cannot rest on a generalized claim that discrimination exists in society or in a particular agency.[66] "A governmental actor cannot render race a legitimate proxy for a particular condition merely by declaring that the condition exists."[67] Indeed, "blind deference to legislative or executive pronouncements of necessity has no place in equal protection analysis."[68]

Second, because the concept of underrepresentation "rests on the completely unrealistic assumption that minorities will choose a particular trade in lockstep proportion to their representation in the local population,"[69] underrepresentation or disparity is not sufficient to establish "a strong basis in evidence" for present effects of racial discrimination that would permit an agency to take race-conscious action to fashion a remedy consistent with the Constitution.[70] "If our society is to continue to progress as a multiracial democracy, it must recognize that the automatic invocation of race stereotypes retards that progress and causes continued hurt and injury."[71]

In this regard, "when special qualifications are required to fill particular jobs, comparisons to the general population (rather than the smaller group of individuals who possess the necessary qualifications) may have little probative value."[72] Accordingly, assertions that minorities make up a specific portion of the population, a specific portion of business owners, or even specific portion of business owners in a particular field become irrelevant. "Where special qualifications are necessary, the relevant statistical pool for purposes of demonstrating discriminatory exclusion must be the number of minorities qualified to undertake the particular task."[73]

Third, there must be "some showing of prior discrimination by the *governmental unit involved.*"[74] If the government "show[s] that it had essentially become a 'passive participant' in a system of racial exclusion practiced by elements of [a] local . . . industry," then the government can act to undo the discrimination.[75] Conversely, "if the government cannot show that it actively or passively participated in this past discrimination, race-based remedial measures violate equal-protection principles."[76]

Fourth, findings of discrimination cannot be extrapolated from one governmental unit to another.[77] "When we begin by assuming that every predominately white college or university discriminated in the past, whether or not true, we are no longer talking about the kind of discrimination for which a race-conscious remedy may be prescribed."[78] Nor can findings of discrimination against one racial group be extrapolated to other racial groups. "The random inclusion of racial groups that, as a practical matter, may never have suffered from discrimination . . . suggests that perhaps the . . . purpose was not in fact to remedy past discrimination."[79] This refusal to extrapolate discrimination from one governmental entity to another is fully consistent with the Court's desegregation jurisprudence.[80]

B. Narrow Tailoring

"Once the University has established that its goal . . . is consistent with strict scrutiny, however, there must still be a further judicial determination that the [University] meets strict scrutiny in its implementation. The University must prove that the means chosen by the University . . . are narrowly tailored to that goal. On this point, the University receives no deference."[81]

Moreover, "the mere recitation of a 'benign' or legitimate purpose for a racial classification is entitled to little or no weight. Strict scrutiny does not permit a court to accept a school's assertion that [it] uses race in a permissible way without a court giving close analysis to the evidence of how the process works in practice."[82] "The purpose of the narrow tailoring requirement is to ensure that 'the means chosen fit . . . th[e] compelling goal so closely that there is little or no possibility that the motive for the classification was illegitimate racial prejudice or stereotype.'"[83] To the extent that "[c]ontext matters when reviewing race-based governmental action under the Equal Protection Clause,"[84] the narrow tailoring "inquiry must be calibrated to fit the distinct issues raised by the use of race to achieve the government's asserted goals."[85] Indeed, the very purpose of strict scrutiny is to consider such relevant differences.[86]

Narrow tailoring involves four factors. First, a serious good faith consideration of race-neutral alternatives. Second, individualized consideration of every person or entity eligible for the program. Third, there cannot be an undue burden on racial groups that are not receiving the preference. Fourth, the use of race must be periodically reviewed and of limited duration. Each of these factors is discussed in detail below.

1. Serious Good Faith Consideration of Racial Neutral Alternatives

For a policy to survive narrow-tailoring analysis, the government must show "serious, good faith consideration of workable race-neutral alternatives."[87] "This requires the government to engage in a genuine effort to determine whether alternative policies could address the alleged harm."[88] A court must not uphold a race-conscious policy unless it is "satisfied that no workable race-neutral alternative" would achieve the compelling interest.[89] "In addition, a policy is not narrowly tailored if it is either overbroad or underinclusive in its use of racial classifications."[90]

In the context of officials at public colleges or universities using race to achieve the educational benefits of a diverse student body, judges must inquire "into whether a university could achieve sufficient diversity without using racial classifications."[91] This means administrators must prove there are "no workable race-neutral alternatives that would produce the educational benefits of diversity."[92] If a workable race-neutral alternative exists, "then the University may not consider race."[93]

This requirement to prove a negative—that no race-neutral alternative would produce the desired level of minority representation—raises significant challenges for institutional officials. Simply put, one cannot determine the viability of a race-neutral alternative without first making assumptions about what level of minority representation is sufficient.

It is not enough to ascertain that a race-neutral alternative will yield a minority representation of X percent, one must know whether X percent is a "critical mass." If X percent is a critical mass, then the race-neutral alternative is viable. In that instance, institutional officials may not consider race. Conversely, if X percent is not a critical mass, then the race-neutral alternative is not workable. In such a situation, the institution may use race.

In these circumstances, the institutional officials' definition of critical mass effectively becomes determinative. While administrators are entitled to deference on whether they need to pursue diversity, they are not entitled to deference on what constitutes a critical mass. Otherwise, institution leaders could simply define critical mass in such a way as to always justify the use of race. For example, if administrators announced they wanted minority representation of 90 percent, it would render all possible race-neutral alternatives unworkable.

While the Supreme Court has not provided guidance on what constitutes a critical mass and while that definition may well depend upon context, certain parameters seem inherent in any definition of critical mass. Just as it is "completely unrealistic" to assume "that minorities will choose a particular trade in lockstep proportion to their representation in the local population,"[94] it is just as unrealistic to assume that minority representation on a particular campus will exceed their representation in the area served by the institution. Thus, if a public institution serves a State or a particular region of a State, the level of minority representation in that State or region provides some rough guidance as to the definition of critical mass. For those public colleges or universities that serve States or regions with low minority populations, it will be difficult to define critical mass as a high number of minorities.

Once critical mass is defined in a constitutional manner, then the institutional officials must demonstrate that there is no realistic race-neutral alternative that can achieve the critical mass. Making such a showing will be difficult. It likely involves an analysis of the impact of automatically admitting the top students at every high school in a State or region. In areas where many high schools are not integrated, such a plan can yield a significant amount of minority representation. Campus officials must also examine socioeconomic preferences. If minorities are a disproportionate share of the poor in the areas served by the institution, then a socioeconomic preference has the potential to increase minority representation. A similar logic applies to first-generation students—applicants who will be the first in their families to attend higher education. Additionally, campus leaders must explore other creative race-neutral measures—such as quotas by region of their States—that might lead to increased minority representation.

For many public institutions, there will be workable race-neutral alternatives. If so, then the institutional leaders must cease using race and start using the race-neutral alternatives. Racial preferences will end at those schools. Conversely, there will be some institutions where there are no workable race-neutral preferences. This latter situation likely will be the case if the minority population is relatively low, if the high schools where minorities attend generally are integrated, and if nonminorities are a sizable portion of the poor and/or the first-generation applicants. Officials at these institutions will be allowed to pursue racial preferences, albeit subject to the significant judicial limitations.

2. Individualized Consideration

Individualized consideration involves two elements.[95] First, the selection process may not "insulate applicants who belong to certain racial or ethnic groups from the competition."[96] Public higher education administrators must treat "each applicant as an individual, and not simply as a member of a particular racial group."[97] Therefore, the institutional policies "cannot establish quotas for members of certain racial groups"[98] and may not reserve "a certain fixed number or proportion of the available opportunities . . . exclusively for certain minority groups."[99] In practical terms, there can be no race exclusive scholarship or special admissions program.[100]

In the context of higher education admissions, the Supreme Court recognized a legally significant difference between the use of a quota and the "goal of attaining a critical mass of underrepresented students."[101] While the Constitution prohibits the former, it allows the latter. On the one hand, "quotas impose a fixed number or percentage which must be attained . . . and insulate the individual from comparison with all other candidates for the available seats."[102] On the other hand, "a permissible goal . . . requires only a good faith effort . . . to come within a range demarcated by the goal itself, and permits consideration of race as a 'plus' factor in any given case while still ensuring that each candidate competes with all other qualified applicants."

Second, race can be neither decisive[103] nor the "defining feature" of an application.[104] To illustrate, consider the pursuit of the educational benefits of a diverse student body. Diversity arises from "*a far broader array* of qualifications and characteristics"[105] and focuses on "those students who will contribute the most to the robust *exchange of ideas*,"[106] Therefore, the Supreme Court "emphasized the importance of considering each particular applicant as an individual, assessing all of the qualities that individual possesses, and in turn, evaluating that individual's ability to contribute to the unique setting of higher education."[107] "Just as growing up in a particular region or having particular professional experiences is likely to affect an individual's views, so too is one's own, unique experience of being a racial minority in a society, like our own, in which race unfortunately still matters."[108]

Of course, such an examination necessarily includes an evaluation of other factors that may shape attitudes and experiences such as one's religion, cultural background, socioeconomic class, or home life. If applicants are to be judged based on the experiences and attitudes that they would bring to the intellectual life of the institution they wish to enter, then an individual's race, like any other factor that shape attitudes and experiences, becomes relevant. Race is not determinative or even dominant, but it is a factor.

3. No Undue Burden for Other Racial Groups

Because "there are serious problems of justice connected with the idea of preference itself,"[109] any racial remedy "must not 'unduly burden individuals who are not members of the favored racial and ethnic groups.'"[110] "Narrow tailoring, therefore, requires that a race-conscious admissions program not unduly harm members of any racial group."[111] Even a remedial race-based governmental action generally "remains subject to continuing oversight to assure that it will work the least harm possible to other innocent persons competing for the benefit."[112] In short, any raced-based remedy adopted by governmental officials cannot create an undue burden or harm on innocent persons who are not part of the group that the policy aims to help.

In previous decisions, the Supreme Court held there was no undue burden on other racial groups when everyone, regardless of race, was considered,[113] or where the remedy was "temporary and extremely limited" and only postponed, rather than denied, opportunities to other racial groups.[114] As a practical matter, this means designating some admissions slots for racial minorities or having a race exclusive scholarship will be considered an undue burden.

4. Limited Duration

Because "a core purpose of the Fourteenth Amendment was to do away with all governmentally imposed discrimination based on race,"[115] the racial remedy "must be limited in time."[116] When it permits racial classification, the judiciary insists that the racial classification end once compelling interest is achieved.[117] The requirement that all race-conscious programs have a termination point "assure[s] all citizens that the deviation from the norm of equal treatment of all racial and ethnic groups is a temporary matter, a measure taken in the service of the goal of equality itself."[118]

"The durational requirement can be met by sunset provisions in race-conscious admissions policies and periodic reviews to determine whether racial preferences are still necessary to" achieve the compelling governmental interest.[119] In 2003, the Supreme Court approved the use of racial preferences by officials at the University of Michigan's law school, but said, "we expect twenty-five years from now, the use of racial preferences will no longer be necessary to further interest approved today."[120]

II. SEX

A. Constitutional Standard

"Like racial classifications, sex-based discrimination is presumptively invalid."[121] Government policies that discriminate based on sex cannot stand unless the government provides an "exceedingly persuasive justification."[122] To survive constitutional review, the government must prove the sex classifications: (1) serve important governmental objectives; and (2) are substantially related to the achievement of those objectives.[123] Each of these requirements deserves additional elaboration as follows.

First, the purpose of the sex classification, the end being pursued, must be an important governmental objective. Just as societal discrimination cannot justify the government's use of a racial classification,[124] societal discrimination cannot justify the government's use a sex classification.[125] This means officials at public colleges and universities "can evoke a compensatory purpose to justify an otherwise discriminatory classification only if members of the gender benefited by the classification actually suffer a disadvantage related to the classification."[126] Stated differently, the officials at the public institution must prove men or women "actually suffer[ed] a disadvantage because of discrimination."[127] "The mere recitation of a benign, compensatory purpose is not an automatic shield which protects against any inquiry into the actual purposes underlying a statutory scheme."[128] "Proving broad sociological propositions by statistics is a dubious business."[129]

Second, the implementation of the sex classification, the means to the end, must be substantially related to the important governmental objectives. "The purpose of requiring that close relationship is to assure that the validity of a classification is determined through concluded analysis rather than through the mechanical application of traditional, often inaccurate, assumptions about the proper roles of men and women."[130]

Two Supreme Court decisions involving public higher education illustrate the working of this constitutional standard. In *Mississippi University for Woman v. Hogan*, the Court held a public institution of higher education could not prohibit men from enrolling in a nursing program.[131] Similarly, in *United States v. Virginia*, the Court held Virginia Military Institute could not exclude women, but also found officials' attempt to create a "comparable single gender institution" for women was a "pale shadow" of the Institute.[132]

Three broad constitutional rules can be gleaned from these cases. First, officials at a public institution of higher education may not exclude individuals from a particular educational program because of an individual's sex. Although the privacy interests and the inherent physical differences between the sexes may require sex segregation in some facilities or programs such as intercollegiate athletics, no person may be excluded totally from participation.

Second, the Equal Protection Clause mandates equal opportunities, not equal outcomes. Just as it is "completely unrealistic" to assume "minorities will choose a particular trade in lockstep proportion to their representation in the local population,"[133] it is completely unrealistic to assume men and women will choose a particular education program in lockstep proportion to their representation in the general population. If men are not excluded, it does not matter that woman constitute a disproportionate share of the enrollment in an institution or in a particular program or major. At the same time, women cannot be denied participation because they are "overrepresented." Put another way, there can be no quotas in educational programs.

Third, where privacy interests and the inherent differences between the sexes require sex segregation, such as student housing and sport, officials at the public institution must ensure that each sex is treated in the same manner. This means officials must provide comparable facilities to both sexes, not mere shadows of each other. If women are housed in residence halls built in the 2010s, the men cannot be confined to residence halls built in the 1960s. If the men's sports teams have high quality coaching, the best equipment, and travel by jet, then the women's teams must receive high quality coaching, the best equipment, and travel by jet.

B. Title IX Generally Codifies the Constitution

Title IX of the Education Amendments of 1972 requires all educational institutions receiving federal funds to refrain from sex discrimination.[134] Title IX is modeled on Title VI of the Civil Rights Act of 1964, which prohibits racial discrimination by recipients of federal funds.[135] Moreover, the "two statutes operate in the same manner, conditioning an offer of federal funding on a promise by the recipient not to discriminate, in what amounts essentially to a contract between the Government and the recipient of funds."[136] In fact, Title VI and Title IX are to be interpreted in the same manner.[137]

Although Supreme Court dicta states Title IX is both broader and narrower than the Equal Protection Clause,[138] the Court has explicitly ruled Title VI is coextensive with the Equal Protection Clause.[139] Because Title VI is coextensive with the Equal Protection Clause, Title IX logically must also be coextensive with the Equal Protection Clause. Thus, any Title IX claim against a public institution is also a constitutional claim for violation of the Equal Protection Clause. Indeed, when a public institution is sued for alleged violations of Title IX, individual administrators may be sued for alleged violations of the Equal Protection Clause.[140]

Put another way, for administrators at public institutions, their constitutional obligations of the Equal Protection Clause and the statutory obligations of Title IX are the same. If Congress were to repeal Title IX, public universities would still have the same obligations. Consequently, judicial interpretations of Title IX provide informative, if not definitive, guidance for equal protection claims involving sex.

Judicial decisions involving sexual harassment/sexual assault are particularly relevant. For example, it is not enough for the administrators to prohibit sexual assault or discipline the perpetrators; officials are required to take measures to prevent sexual assault and lessen its impact on individual students.[141] Under the Equal Protection Clause, once responsible officials at public institutions learn of a sexual assault, they must respond in a manner that is not clearly unreasonable.[142]

In the context of employee-student sexual harassment/sexual assault, a violation of Title IX, and by extension, the Equal Protection Clause, has two elements. First, a campus official "who at a minimum has authority to address the alleged discrimination and to institute corrective measures" on the institution's behalf must have actual notice, not constructive notice, of the conduct.[143] Second, having knowledge of the alleged harassment, the administrator responds with "deliberate indifference."[144] "The premise, in other words, is an official decision by the [university] not to remedy the violation."[145] Yet, it is not necessary to terminate every faculty member who engages in sexual harassment.[146]

If the sexual harassment/sexual assault involves two students rather than a student and an employee, there is a third element: officials must exercise "substantial control over both the harasser and the context in which the known harassment occurs."[147] While officials in public institutions have substantial control over what takes place in classrooms or laboratories and perhaps what happens even in a residence hall, whether they have substantial control over off campus locations will depend upon the individual facts and circumstances of the alleged incidents.

III. SEXUAL ORIENTATION

Although contemporary American society tends to view sexual orientation as an immutable characteristic like race or sex, classifications involving sexual orientation are not subject to the heightened scrutiny used in race or sex cases. Instead, the Supreme Court will uphold a sexual orientation "classification so long as it bears a rational relation to some legitimate end."[148] While this standard normally is highly deferential to the Legislative and Executive Branches, the Court has refused to defer when sexual orientation classifications are involved.[149]

To illustrate, the Supreme Court invalidated a Colorado State Constitutional Amendment that prevented state and local governments from enacting statutes and ordinances prohibiting discrimination based on sexual orientation. The Court found the provision imposed "a broad and undifferentiated disability on a single named group, an exceptional and . . . invalid form of legislation"[150] and had no purpose but to "deem a class of persons a stranger to its laws."[151] In subsequent cases involving differing treatment based on sexual orientation, the Court has focused not on the classification, but on fundamental rights to sexual privacy[152] and marriage[153] as well as the federal government's authority over marriage.[154]

As a practical matter, the Constitution prohibits officials at public institutions from treating people differently because of their sexual orientations. There is no rational reason to deny admission or employment to individuals who are gay or lesbian. Similarly, there is no rational reason for excluding individuals from a scholarship program simply because of their sexual orientation.

The Supreme Court's decisions involve gays and lesbians, and have not addressed transgender individuals or others who are part of the LGBTQIA+

community. While the Court found gender identity discrimination to be "sex" discrimination for the purposes of Title VII,[155] a federal employment statute,[156] it is unclear whether gender identity discrimination is "sex" discrimination for purposes of the Constitution. Future decisions may provide further guidance on this issue.

In any event, even if gender identity discrimination is not "sex" discrimination for constitutional purposes, there is no rational reason to deny admission or employment to a transgender individual or any other persons who are part of the LGBTQIA+ community.

IV. ALIENAGE

"As a general matter, a state law that discriminates on the basis of alienage can be sustained only if . . . the law must advance a compelling state interest by the least restrictive means available."[157] This means a State, including a public institution of higher education, may not bar aliens from pursuing civil service positions[158] or pursuing certain professions.[159]

Yet, the Supreme Court has established a "political function" exception that allows States to "exclude aliens from positions intimately related to the process of democratic self-government."[160] "The rationale behind the political-function exception is that within broad boundaries a State may establish its own form of government and limit the right to govern to those who are full-fledged members of the political community."[161] Because some positions "are so closely bound up with the formulation and implementation of self-government that the State is permitted to exclude from those positions persons outside the political community."[162]

In determining whether this political-function exception applies, the Supreme Court asks two questions.[163] "First, the specificity of the classification will be examined: a classification that is substantially overinclusive or underinclusive tends to undercut the governmental claim that the classification serves legitimate political ends."[164] "Second, even if the classification is sufficiently tailored, it may be applied in the particular case only to persons holding state elective or important nonelective executive, legislative, and judicial positions" who "perform functions that go to the heart of representative government."[165] This allows States to exclude aliens from serving as police officers,[166] probation officers,[167] or K–12 public school teachers.[168]

V. DISABILITY

In *Cleburne v. Cleburne Living Center, Inc.*, the Supreme Court ruled classifications based on disorders of intellectual development were not subject to heightened scrutiny.[169] The Court concluded, "it would be difficult to find a principled way to distinguish a variety of other groups who have perhaps immutable disabilities setting them off from others, who cannot themselves mandate the desired legislative responses, and who can claim some degree of prejudice from at least part of the public at large."[170] Instead, the Court upheld such classifications as permissible as long as the underlying statutes or policies are rationally related to a legitimate state interest.[171]

Although *Cleburne* involved disorders of intellectual development, the Supreme Court has subsequently declared all classifications based on disability, whether physical or intellectual, are subject to rational basis review.[172] The exact contours of rational basis review are discussed below in the part of this chapter devoted to other characteristics.

Because both federal and state law impose restrictions on disability discrimination that go beyond the Equal Protection Clause, individuals with disabilities may have a statutory claim rather than constitutional claims. A discussion of these statutory provisions is well beyond the scope of this book.

VI. OTHER CHARACTERISTICS

The Equal Protection Clause's "promise that no person shall be denied the equal protection of the laws must coexist with the practical necessity that most legislation classifies for one purpose or another, with resulting disadvantage to various groups or persons."[173] For example, if officials at a public campus limit admission to applicants with high test scores and high grades, they necessarily discriminate against those with low test scores and low grades. A similar dynamic exists in every classroom, laboratory, or a playing field.

As explained earlier in this chapter, laws or policies that discriminate based on race, sex, or alienage are subject to heightened scrutiny. In all other cases, "a law will be sustained if it can be said to advance a legitimate government interest, even if the law seems unwise or works to the disadvantage of a particular group, or if the rationale for it seems tenuous."[174] "By requiring that the classification bear a rational relationship to an independent and legitimate legislative end," the Supreme Court can be certain "classifications are not drawn for the purpose of disadvantaging the group burdened by the law."[175]

Under this deferential rational basis standard, the parties challenging the statutes or policies bear the burden "to negat[e] every conceivable basis which might support" the legislation.[176] Additionally, officials at public campuses have no obligation to produce evidence to support the rationality of statutes, which "may be based on rational speculation unsupported by any evidence or empirical data."[177]

Rather, "a State does not violate the Equal Protection Clause merely because the classifications made by its laws are imperfect."[178] As long as there is a rational basis for the statute or policy, "it does not offend the Constitution simply because the classification 'is not made with mathematical nicety or because in practice it results in some inequality.'"[179] The Supreme Court has declared, "a legislative choice is not subject to courtroom fact-finding," and "equal protection [analysis] is not a license for the courts to judge the wisdom, fairness, or logic of the legislative choices."[180] Thus, legislation is valid even though there may be an imperfect fit between means and ends.[181]

VII. SUMMARY OF THE MAJOR CASES DISCUSSED IN THIS CHAPTER

Adarand Constructors v. Peña, 515 U.S. 200 (1995)

The Supreme Court held that federal government's use of racial preferences was subject to the same constitutional standards as a state or local government's use of racial preferences. Therefore, the Court invalidated a federal program designed to offer contracts to disadvantaged businesses because its use of race was not sufficiently narrowly tailored to achieve a compelling governmental interest.

City of Cleburne v. Cleburne Living Center, 473 U.S. 432 (1985)

The Supreme Court ruled that classifications related to disorders of intellectual development were not subject to heightened scrutiny. Rather, such differing treatment would be upheld if it were rationally related to a legitimate governmental interest.

City of Richmond v. J.A. Croson Co., 488 U.S. 469 (1989)

The Supreme Court found a state or local government could not use a racial preference except the use of race was narrowly tailored to achieving the compelling governmental interest of remedying the present-day effects of past intentional discrimination by the governmental entity. As a result, the Court invalidated a minority set-aside provision for governmental contracts because city officials in Virginia failed to demonstrate a compelling governmental interest justifying the plan and it was not sufficiently narrowly tailored to remedy the effects of prior discrimination.

Davis v. Monroe County Board of Education, 526 U.S. 629 (1999)

The Supreme Court decided an educational entity which receives federal funds has liability for student-on-student sexual harassment under Title IX if it has actual knowledge of the harassment, responds with deliberate indifference, and has substantial control over both the harasser and the context where the harassment occurs. The Court also defined harassment as conduct or expression so severe, pervasive, and objectively offensive that it effectively bars the victim's access to an educational opportunity or benefit.

Fisher v. University of Texas, 570 U.S. 297 (2013) (*Fisher I*)

The Supreme Court determined lower courts improperly applied the constitutional standard for evaluating the constitutionality of an admissions program designed to increase minority enrollment. In doing so, the Court clarified the constitutional standard for evaluating racial preferences. Accordingly, the Court remanded the case for further consideration.

Fisher v. University of Texas, 136 S. Ct. 2198 (2016) (*Fisher II*)

The Supreme Court concluded a state university's policy, which was unique in that it guaranteed the admission of top students at every high school but continued to use race as one factor among many, was consistent with the Constitution.

Gebser v. Lago Vista Independent School District, 524 U.S. 274 (1998)

The Supreme Court held that an educational entity which receives federal funds has liability for employee on student sexual harassment under Title IX if it has actual knowledge of the harassment and responds with deliberate indifference.

Gratz v. Bollinger, 539 U.S. 244 (2003)

The Supreme Court decided a public university's reliance on a point system in admissions to undergraduate programs where its use of race was insufficiently narrowly tailored to achieve the compelling governmental interest of obtaining the educational benefits of a diverse student body. If an institution is going to use race, the decision establishes the need to evaluate every application on a holistic basis.

Grutter v. Bollinger, 539 U.S. 306 (2003)

The Supreme Court held (1) achieving the educational benefits of a diverse student body was a compelling governmental interest that could justify the use of race; and (2) the University of Michigan's law school's holistic review process for admissions was narrowly tailored to achieve that compelling governmental interest.

Mississippi University for Women v. Hogan, 458 U.S. 718 (1982)

The Supreme Court determined a public institution could not deny admission simply because of the student's sex. The case applied the heightened scrutiny standard requiring sex classifications to be justified by a substantial relationship to an important governmental interest, sex classification.

Parents Involved in Community Schools v. Seattle School District No. 1, 551 U.S. 701 (2007)

The Supreme Court held racial diversity in K-12 education was not a compelling governmental interest. In so ruling, the Court invalidated the use of racial classifications in student assignment plans in Seattle and Louisville.

Romer v. Evans, 517 U.S. 620 (1996)

The Supreme Court decided the People of a State could not amend their State Constitution to prohibit state and local governments from enacting legislation to prohibit sexual orientation discrimination. While the Court found classifications based on sexual orientation were permissible if rationally related to a legitimate state interest, it found the state constitutional amendment to be irrational. The case is the beginning of the Court's recognition of LGBTQIA+ rights.

Regents of the University of California v. Bakke, 438 U.S. 265 (1978)

The Supreme Court determined a state university could not set-aside admissions opportunities for minority applicants. Rather, all applicants must compete for all opportunities. However, a portion of Justice Powell's opinion, which was not joined by any other Justice, suggested race could be one factor among many as a means of obtaining the educational benefits of a diverse student body.

United States v. Virginia, 518 U.S. 515 (1996)

The Supreme Court concluded state officials could not exclude women from a citizen-soldier program. The Court also said a separate and similar program for women only was inadequate to guarantee equal opportunities.

NOTES

1. *Romer v. Evans*, 517 U.S. 620, 623 (1996).
2. U.S. Const. amend. XIV, § 1.
3. *City of Cleburne v. Cleburne Living Center*, 473 U.S. 432, 439 (1985).
4. *Adarand Constructors, Inc. v. Peña*, 515 U.S. 200, 227 (1995) (emphasis in original); *City of Richmond v. J.A. Croson Co.* 488 U.S. 469, 494 (1989); *Wygant v. Jackson Board of Education*, 476 U.S. 267, 279–80 (1986) (Powell, J., joined by Burger, C.J., Rehnquist, J.).
5. Shelley v. Kraemer, 334 U.S. 1, 22 (1948).
6. *Wright v. Rockefeller*, 376 U.S. 52, 66 (1964) (Douglas, J., dissenting).
7. *Regents of the University of California v. Bakke*, 438 U.S. 265, 289–90 (1978).
8. *Romer*, 517 U.S. at 623.
9. *Massachusetts Board of Retirement v. Murgia*, 427 U.S. 307, 314 (1976).
10. *Personnel Adm'r of Massachusetts v. Feeney*, 442 U.S. 256, 271–72 (1979).
11. *Cleburne*, 473 U.S. at 440; *Schweiker v. Wilson*, 450 U.S. 221, 230 (1981).
12. *Cleburne*, 473 U.S. at 440-41; *Graham v. Richardson*, 403 U.S. 365 (1971); *Kramer v. Union Free School District No. 15*, 395 U.S. 621 (1969).
13. *Clark v. Jeter*, 486 U.S. 456, 461 (1988).
14. *Id.*
15. *Id.*
16. *Id.*
17. *Vitolo v. Guzman*, 999 F.3d 353, 360 (6th Cir. 2021).
18. *Rice v. Cayetano*, 528 U.S. 495, 517 (2000).
19. *Shaw v. Reno*, 509 U.S. 630, 643 (1993) (quoting *Hirabayashi v. United States*, 320 U.S. 81, 100 (1943)).
20. *Bolling v. Sharpe*, 347 U.S. 497, 499 (1954).
21. *Croson*, 488 U.S. at 493. (O'Connor, J., joined by Rehnquist, C.J., White and Kennedy, JJ., announcing the judgment of the Court).
22. *United Jewish Orgs. of Williamsburg, Inc. v. Carey*, 430 U.S. 144, 172 (1977) (Brennan, J., concurring).
23. *Grutter v. Bollinger*, 539 U.S. 306. 326 (2003).
24. *Adarand*, 505 U.S. at 227.

25. *Croson Co.,* 488 U.S. at 505 (quoting *Fullilove v. Klutznick,* 448 U.S. 448, 533–34 (1980) (Stevens, J., dissenting)).
26. *Grutter,* 539 U.S. at 326 (citations omitted).
27. *Parents Involved in Community Schools v. Seattle School District No. 1,* 551 U.S. 701, 720 (2007).
28. *Id.* at 748 (Roberts, C.J., joined by Scalia, Thomas, & Alito, JJ., announcing the judgment of the Court).
29. *Mississippi University for Women v. Hogan,* 458 U.S. 718, 724 n. 9 (1982).
30. *Croson,* 488 U.S. at 500.
31. *Adarand,* 515 U.S. at 226.
32. *Johnson v. California,* 543 U.S. 499, 505 (2005).
33. *Adarand,* 505 U.S. at 240 (Thomas, J., concurring).
34. *Id.*
35. *Id.*
36. *Lyng v. Automobile Workers,* 485 U.S. 360, 370 (1988).
37. *F.C.C. v. Beach Commissions, Inc.,* 508 U.S. 307, 314–15 (1993) (Quoting *Lehnhausen v. Lake Shore Auto Parts Co.,* 410 U.S. 356, 364 (1973)).
38. *Johnson,* 543 U.S. at 505 (Quoting *Adarand,* 515 U.S. at 227).
39. *Grutter,* 539 U.S. at 328–30.
40. *Croson,* 488 U.S. at 504–05.
41. *Shaw v. Hunt,* 517 U.S. 899, 909–10 (1996); *Croson* 488 U.S. at 498–99; *Wygant,* 476 U.S. at 276 (Powell, J, joined by Burger, C.J., White, & Rehnquist, JJ, announcing the judgment of the Court); *id.* at 288 (O'Connor, J., concurring).
42. *Parents Involved,* 551 U.S. at 731 (Roberts, J., joined by Scalia, Thomas, and Alito, JJ. announcing the judgment of the Court).
43. *Id.* (Roberts, J., joined by Scalia, Thomas, and Alito, JJ. announcing the judgment of the Court); *Wygant,* 476 U.S. at 276 (Powell, J, joined by Burger, C.J., White, & Rehnquist, JJ, announcing the judgment of the Court).
44. *Croson,* 488 U.S. at 507 (quoting *Sheet Metal Workers v. E.E.O.C.,* 478 U.S. 421, 494 (1986) (O'Connor, J., concurring in part and dissenting in part)).
45. *Grutter,* 539 U.S. at 323–24; *Wygant,* 476 U.S. at 267 (Powell, J, joined by Burger, C.J., White, & Rehnquist, JJ, announcing the judgment of the Court), *Bakke,* 438 U.S. at 307–10.
46. *Bakke,* 438 U.S. at 310–11 (Powell, J., announcing the judgment of the Court).
47. *Croson,* 488 U.S. at 505–506.
48. *Bakke,* 438 U.S., at 315 (Powell, J., announcing the judgment of the court).
49. *Fisher v. University of Texas at Austin,* 570 U.S. 297, 311 (2013).
50. *Grutter,* 539 U.S, at 330.
51. *Parents Involved,* 551 U.S. at 732.
52. *Grutter,* 539 U.S. at 343–44.
53. *Id.* at 324.
54. *Bakke,* 438 U.S., at 315 (Powell, J., announcing the judgment of the court).
55. *Grutter,* 539 U.S. at 330.
56. *Keyishian v. Board of Regents of University of State of New York,* 385 U.S. 589, 603 (1967).

57. *Bakke*, 438 U.S. at 312 (1978) (Powell, J., announcing the judgment of the Court).

58. *Grutter*, 539 U.S. at 333 (citations omitted).

59. Eli I. Capilouto, Address to the Lexington, Kentucky Martin Luther King Day Celebration (2016).

60. Greg Lukianoff, UNLEARNING LIBERTY: CAMPUS CENSORSHIP AND THE END OF AMERICAN DEBATE 33 (2012).

61. *Croson*, 488 U.S. at 510–11 (O'Connor, J., joined by Rehnquist, C.J., White and Kennedy, JJ., announcing the judgment of the Court).

62. *Id.* at 500.

63. *Id.* at 510–11 (O'Connor, J., joined by Rehnquist, C.J., White and Kennedy, JJ., announcing the judgment of the Court).

64. *Id.*

65. *Williamson v. Lee Optical Co.*, 348 U.S. 483, 488–89 (1955).

66. *McLaughlin v. Florida*, 379 U.S. 184, 190–92 (1964).

67. *Croson*, 488 U.S. at 500–01 (citations omitted).

68. *Id.* at 500–501.

69. *Id.* at 507 (quoting *Sheet Metal Workers v. E.E.O.C.*, 478 U.S. 421, 494 (1986) (O'Connor, J., concurring in part and dissenting in part)).

70. *Washington v. Davis*, 426 U.S. 229, 250–52 (1976); *Mayor of Philadelphia v. Education Equity League*, 415 U.S. 605, 620 (1974).

71. *Edmonson v. Leesville Concrete Co.*, 500 U.S. 614, 630 (1991).

72. *Croson*, 488 U.S. at 501 (quoting *Hazelwood School District v. United States*, 433 U.S. 299, 308 n.13 (1977)).

73. *Id.* at 501–2.

74. *Wygant*, 476 U.S. at 274 (Powell, J., joined by Burger, C.J., Rehnquist & O'Connor, JJ., announcing the judgment of the Court).

75. *Croson.*, 488 U.S. at 492 11 (O'Connor, J., joined by Rehnquist, C.J., White and Kennedy, JJ., announcing the judgment of the Court).

76. *Vitalo*, 999 F.3d at 361.

77. *Croson*, 488 U.S. at 508.

78. *Podberesky v. Kirwan*, 38 F.3d 146, 155 (4th Cir. 1994).

79. *Croson*, 488 U.S. at 506.

80. *Missouri v. Jenkins*, 515 U.S. 70, 88 (1995); *Milliken v. Bradley*, 418 U.S. 717, 746 (1974).

81. *Fisher*, 570 U.S. at 311.

82. *Id.* at 313.

83. *Grutter*, 539 U.S. at 333.

84. *Id.* at 327.

85. *Id.* at 333–34.

86. *Adarand*, 515 U.S. at 226–28.

87. *Grutter*, 539 U.S. at 339; *Croson*, 488 U.S. at 507.

88. *Vitolo*, 999 F.3d at 362.

89. *Fisher*, 570 U.S. at 312.

90. *Vitolo*, 999 F.3d at 362–63.

91. *Fisher*, 570 U.S. at 311.
92. *Id.*
93. *Id.*
94. *Croson*, 488 U.S. at 507.
95. *Grutter*, 539 U.S. at 336.
96. *Id.* at 334.
97. *Parents Involved*, 551 U.S. at 722.
98. *Grutter*, 539 U.S. at 309.
99. *Id.* at 334.
100. *Podberesky*, 38 F.3d at 155.
101. *Grutter*, 539 U.S. at 336.
102. *Id.* at 348.
103. *Gratz v. Bollinger*, 539 U.S. 244, 271 (2003).
104. *Grutter*, 539 U.S. at 336.
105. *Id.* at 324.
106. *Bakke*, 438 U.S. at 313 (Powell, J., announcing the judgment of the Court).
107. *Gratz*, 539 U.S. at 271.
108. *Id.*
109. *Bakke*, 438 U.S., at 298 (Powell, J., announcing the judgment of the Court).
110. *Grutter*, 539 U.S. at 341 (quoting *Metro Broadcasting, Inc. v. FCC*, 497 U.S. 547, 630 (1990) (O'Connor, J., joined by Rehnquist, C.J, Scalia, & Kennedy, JJ., dissenting)).
111. *Grutter*, 539 U.S. at 341.
112. *Bakke*, 438 U.S. at 308 (Powell, J., announcing the judgment of the Court).
113. *Grutter*, 539 U.S. at 341.
114. *United States v. Paradise*, 480 U.S. 149, 182–83 (1987) (Brennan, J., joined by Marshall, Blackmun, & Powell, JJ., announcing the judgment of the Court).
115. *Palmore v. Sidoti*, 466 U.S. 429, 432, (1984).
116. *Grutter*, 539 U.S. at 342. *See also Paradise*, 480 U.S. at 178.
117. *Parents Involved*, 551 U.S. at 744.
118. *Croson*, 488 U.S. at 510 (O'Connor, J., joined by joined by Rehnquist, C.J., White and Kennedy, JJ., announcing the judgment of the Court).
119. *Grutter*, 539 U.S. at 342.
120. *Id.* at 343.
121. *Vitolo*, 999 F.3d at 364.
122. *United States v. Virginia*, 518 U.S. 515, 531 (1996).
123. *Mississippi University for Women v. Hogan*, 458 U.S. 718, 724,730 (1982); *Craig v. Boren*, 429 U.S. 190, 197 (1976).
124. *Shaw v. Hunt*, 517 U.S. 899, 909–10 (1996); *Wygant*, 476 U.S. at 274–75.
125. *Hogan*, 458 U.S. at 727–29.
126. *Id.* at 728.
127. *Id.*
128. *Weinberger v. Wiesenfeld*, 420 U.S. 636, 648 (1975).
129. *Boren*, 429 U.S. at 200–204.
130. *Hogan*, 458 U.S. at 725–26.

131. *Id.* at 731.
132. *Virginia*, 518 U.S. at 553.
133. *Croson*, 488 U.S. at 507 (quoting *Sheet Metal Workers v. E.E.O.C.*, 478 U.S. 421, 494 (1986) (O'Connor, J., concurring in part and dissenting in part)).
134. 20 U.S.C. § 1681 et seq.
135. 42 U.S.C. §§ 2000d–2000d-7.
136. *Gebser v. Lago Vista Indep. School District*, 524 U.S. 274, 286 (1998).
137. *Cannon v. University of Chi.*, 441 U.S. 677, 694–96 (1979).
138. *Fitzgerald v. Barnstable School Comm.*, 555 U.S. 246, 256 (2009).
139. *Alexander v. Sandoval*, 532 U.S. 275, 280–81 (2001).
140. *Fitzgerald*, 555 U.S. at 258.
141. Diane L. Rosenfeld, *Uncomfortable Conversations: Confronting the Reality of Target Rape on Campus*, 128 Harv. L. Rev. F. 359, 369 (2015); Stephen Henrick, *A Hostile Environment for Student Defendants: Title IX and Sexual Assault on College Campuses*, 40 N. Ky. L. Rev. 49, 52 (2013).
142. *Davis v. Monroe County. Board of Education*, 526 U.S. 629, 644–47 (1999).
143. *Gebser*, 524 U.S. at 289–91.
144. *Id.* at 291–92.
145. *Id.*, at 291.
146. *Davis*, 526 U.S. at 648.
147. *Id.* at 645.
148. *Romer*, 517 U.S. at 631.
149. *Id.* at 632.
150. *Id.*
151. *Id.* at 636.
152. *Lawrence v. Texas*, 539 U.S. 558 (2003).
153. *Obergefell v. Hodges*, 576 U.S. 644 (2015).
154. *United States v. Windsor*, 570 U.S. 744 (2013).
155. 42 U.SC. § 2000 et. seq.
156. *Bostock v. Clayton County*, 140 S. Ct. 1731 (2020).
157. *Bernal v. Fainter*, 467 U.S. 216, 219 (1984).
158. *Sugarman v. Dougall*, 413 U.S. 634 (1973).
159. *Examining Board v. Flores de Otero*, 426 U.S. 572 (1976); *In re Griffiths*, 413 U.S. 717 (1973).
160. *Bernal*, 467 U.S. at 220.
161. *Id.* at 221.
162. *Id.*
163. *Id.* at 222.
164. *Cabell v. Chavez-Salido*, 454 U.S. 432, 440 (1982).
165. *Id.* at 440.
166. *Foley v. Connelie*, 435 U.S. 291, 297 (1978).
167. *Cabell*, 454 U.S. 442–44.
168. *Ambach v. Norwick*, 441 U.S. 68, 78–79 (1979).
169. *Cleburne*, 473 U.S. at 445–46.
170. *Id.* at 445.

171. *Id.* at 446.
172. *Board. of Trustees of the University of Alabama v. Garrett*, 531 U.S. 356, 366–67 (2001).
173. *Romer*, 517 U.S. at 631.
174. *Id.* at 632.
175. *Id.* at 633.
176. *Lehnhausen v. Lake Shore Auto Parts Co.*, 410 U.S. 356, 364 (1973).
177. *FCC v. Beach Communications, Inc.*, 508 U.S. 307, 315 (1993).
178. *Dandridge v. Williams*, 397 U.S. 471, 485 (1970).
179. *Id.*
180. *Beach Communications, Inc.*, 508 U.S. at 313.
181. *Heller v. Doe*, 509 U.S. 312, 321 (1993).

Chapter 4

A Fundamental Value Determination

Procedural Due Process in Campus Disciplinary Proceedings

> It still remains "a fundamental value determination of our society that it is far worse to convict an innocent man than to let a guilty man go free."—*Arizona v. Youngblood*[1]

Unlike the legal traditions of other cultures, the Anglo-American-Australasian legal tradition has required procedural due process before government deprives an individual of life, liberty, or property.[2] The focus is on preventing the government from making mistakes—it is better for ten guilty men to go free than for an innocent man to be imprisoned.[3] "If, for example, the standard of proof for a criminal trial were a preponderance of the evidence rather than proof beyond a reasonable doubt, there would be a smaller risk of factual errors that result in freeing guilty persons, but a far greater risk of factual errors that result in convicting the innocent."[4] All doubts must be resolved in favor of the individual.[5]

Americans tend to think of due process in terms of criminal proceedings. Yet, it is also a fundamental value determination when the government, including a state university, seeks to deprive an individual of a property or liberty interest, The Due Process Clause requires the government, including officials at public colleges or universities, to provide procedural due process when depriving the individual of a property or liberty interest. For public institutions of higher education, procedural due process becomes important when the institutional officials seek to discipline a student, an employee with civil service protections, or a faculty member.

Nevertheless, "the procedural component of the Due Process Clause does not protect everything that might be described as a 'benefit.'"[6] The "standard analysis" requires courts "first ask whether there exists a liberty or property interest of which a person has been deprived, and if so [courts] ask whether the procedures followed by the State were constitutionally sufficient."[7]

This three-part chapter discusses the Court's analytical framework. Part I discusses whether a specific interest is a constitutionally protected property or liberty interest. Part II examines the requirements of due process. Part III summarizes the major cases discussed in this chapter.

I. IDENTIFYING A CONSTITUTIONALLY PROTECTED PROPERTY OR LIBERTY INTERESTS

"To have a property interest in a benefit, a person clearly must have more than an abstract need or desire for it. He must have more than a unilateral expectation of it. He must, instead, have a legitimate claim of entitlement to it."[8] Conversely, a "benefit is not a protected entitlement if government officials may grant or deny it in their discretion."[9] "Although the underlying substantive interest is created by an independent source such as state law, federal constitutional law determines whether that interest rises to the level of a legitimate claim of entitlement protected by the Due Process Clause."[10]

"The Supreme Court has . . . held that tenured professors at public institutions have a protected property interest in their continued appointment,"[11] but faculty members generally do not have a protected property interest in their administrative assignment as department chair.[12] Faculty members generally do not have any protected property interest in teaching specific classes.[13] Nor does the initiation of termination proceedings constitute a deprivation of a property interest.[14]

Similarly, if an employee who works at a public institution is not on "at will" status, but has state created civil service protections, then the individual has a constitutional protected property interest in continued employment.[15]

With respect to students, since the landmark decision in *Dixon v. Alabama State Board of Education*,[16] it has been clear the Constitution requires due process before officials at a public college or university expel a student or impose a lengthy disciplinary suspension.[17]

While property interests generally are easily identifiable, liberty interests are somewhat more amorphous. The most common liberty interest in higher education occurs when "person's good name, reputation, honor, or integrity is at stake because of what the government is doing to him."[18] However, mere "injury to reputation by itself [is] not a 'liberty' interest protected under the Fourteenth Amendment."[19] In addition to the reputational injury or "stigma," there must be a deprivation of "some more tangible interests" such as loss of employment or expulsion.[20] Thus, if the dismissal of employees involves statements about the individuals' reputations, the employees may well have a liberty interest such that a name clearing hearing is required.

II. ELEMENTS OF DUE PROCESS

While the "Due Process Clause is implicated by higher education disciplinary decisions,"[21] the exact contours of due process depend upon the context.[22] If the property or liberty interest is high, greater protections are required. Conversely, if the property or liberty interests are low, then due process may consist of nothing more than notice and opportunity to be heard.[23]

The Supreme Court has identified three factors that are relevant to identifying the specific dictates of due process. First, what is the individual's interest? Second, what is the risk of a mistaken deprivation of that interest through the procedures being used? Relatedly, are there added safeguards that would lessen this risk. Third, what is the government's interest, including the burdens of using added safeguards?[24]

Although the Supreme Court has never addressed the issue, when officials at public colleges and universities attempt to revoke the tenure of a faculty member or expel a student, the individuals probably are entitled to some sort of hearing.[25] Yet, campus disciplinary hearings "are not criminal trials, and therefore need not take on many of those formalities."[26] At the hearing "the accused has a right to be present for all significant portions of the hearing," but "hearings need not be open to the public."[27] "[N]either rules of evidence nor rules of civil or criminal procedure need be applied."[28] In fact, "witnesses need not be placed under oath."[29] As long as officials at public colleges and universities meet the constitutional standards, they need not follow its own internal procedures and rules in order to satisfy their constitutional obligations.[30]

Officials at public colleges or universities are not required to provide an attorney for a student facing expulsion or a faculty member facing termination of their employees,[31] but institutional officials cannot prohibit individuals from seeking legal counsel.[32] Nor can the officials prohibit an attorney from being present at the hearing and offering advice as a *passive* participant.[33] Still, except where necessary to preserve an individual's,[34] due process does not necessarily require the *active* participation of attorneys in hearings.[35]

Because "[c]ross-examination is the principal means by which the believability of a witness and the truth of his testimony are tested,"[36] some form of cross-examination likely is required in those situations where the "the university's determination turns on the credibility of the accuser, the accused, or witnesses."[37] While recognizing the importance of cross-examination, the appellate courts are divided on exactly how cross-examinations are conducted.[38] Some courts require cross-examinations by students or faculty members or their representatives.[39] Others believe cross-examinations by the presiding hearing officer is sufficient.[40]

"Courts have consistently held that there is no right to an appeal from an academic disciplinary hearing that satisfies due process,"[41] but granting an appeal allows campus officials to correct "any such error that might have occurred, even in proceedings satisfying due process."[42] As the Supreme Court observed, "[t]he risk of error is not at all trivial, and it should be guarded against if that may be done without prohibitive cost or interference with the educational process."[43] Consequently, even though no court has explicitly ruled that an appeal is required, the Constitution would seem to require an appeal.

Such an appeal must be meaningful and not a mere rubber stamp. Like any enterprise run by human beings, "[d]isciplinary hearings, of course, are not flawless."[44] The appellate tribunal must carefully examine whether the accused had access to all the evidence, enjoyed the presumption of innocence, and was able to meaningfully cross-examine witnesses in some form. While a tribunal should review findings of fact for clear error, appellate review for all legal conclusions should be de novo.[45] Should an appellate tribunal conclude that there is a reversible error, then the finding of responsibility must be vacated.[46] If officials of the public institution believe they can prove the violation in another proceeding, then they should attempt to do so.

III. SUMMARY OF MAJOR CASES DISCUSSED IN THIS CHAPTER

Board of Regents of State Colleges v. Roth, 408 U.S. 564 (1972)

The Supreme Court held that faculty members sometimes had a constitutionally protected property interest in their employment or a liberty interest in their reputation. However, in this instance, the Court found the institution's government boards did not violate the Fourteenth Amendment property rights of a faculty member in Wisconsin on a one-year term contract in refusing to provide him with a reason as to why his contract was not renewed.

Dixon v. Alabama State Board of Education, 294 F.2d 150 (5th Cir. 1961)

The Fifth Circuit declared public university students had both constitutionally protected property interest and a liberty interest in enrollment. Therefore, the students were entitled to procedural due process before being expelled or subjected to a lengthy suspension. While the Supreme Court has never addressed the issue, virtually all the other federal Circuits have reached the same result. *Dixon* was the first decision to do so.

Doe v. Baum, 903 F.3d 575 (6th Cir. 2018)

The Sixth Circuit found due process in a student expulsion/suspension hearing required cross-examination and the cross-examination must be conducted by the student or the student's representative. The case is significant for requiring cross-examination in student disciplinary proceeding and for insisting the cross-examination be conducted by the student or the student's representative. Subsequent federal trial court decisions have extended this requirement to faculty disciplinary proceedings.

Goss v. Lopez, 419 U.S. 565 (1975)

The Supreme Court ruled students in K-12 schools facing suspension of ten days or less must be afforded oral or written notice of the charges against them and, if they deny them, explanations of the evidence against them and opportunities to present their sides of the stories. The case establishes procedural due process rights for K-12 students.

Haidak v. University of Massachusetts-Amherst, 933 F.3d 56 (1st Cir. 2019)

The First Circuit determined due process in a student expulsion/suspension hearing required cross-examination in some form. However, the First Circuit rejected the Sixth Circuit's view that the student or the student's representative must conduct cross-examination. Put another way, while cross-examination is required, due process does not require the cross-examination to be conducted by the student or the student's representative.

Paul v. Davis, 424 U.S. 693 (1976)

The Supreme Court decided a government official's defamation of a private citizen, by itself, did not implicate liberty or property interests sufficient to invoke the procedural protections of the Fourteenth Amendment's due process clause. As a result, the citizen could not recover damages on a Section 1983 claim.

Regents of the University of Michigan v. Ewing, 474 U.S. 214 (1985)

The Supreme Court held university officials did not violate a student's substantive due process rights when a faculty board dismissed him from a program without affording him the opportunity to retake a medical board examination that he failed.

NOTES

1. *Arizona v. Youngblood*, 488 U.S. 51, 73, (1988) (quoting *in re Winship*, 397 U.S. 358, 372 (1970) (Harlan, J., concurring).
2. Amalia D. Kessler, *Our Inquisitorial Tradition: Equity Procedure, Due Process, and the Search for an Alternative to the Adversarial*, 90 Cornell L. Rev. 1181, 1211–12 (2005); Belinda Wells & Michael Burnett, *When Cultures Collide: An Australian Citizen's Power to Demand the Death Penalty Under Islamic Law*, 22 Sydney L. Rev. 5, 19 (2000).
3. 2 William Blackstone, Commentaries *358 (1765).
4. *In re* Winship, 397 U.S. at 371 (Harlan, J., concurring).
5. Henry L. Chambers, Jr., *Reasonable Certainty and Reasonable Doubt*, 81 Marq. L. Rev. 655, 658–59 (1998).
6. *Town of Castle Rock, Colo. v. Gonzales*, 545 U.S. 748, 756 (2005).
7. *Swarthout v. Cooke*, 562 U.S. 216, 219 (2011).
8. *Board of Regents of State Colleges v. Roth*, 408 U.S. 564, 577 (1972).
9. *Castle Rock*, 545 U.S. at 756.
10. *Id.* at 757.
11. *Kaplan v. University of Louisville*, 10 F.4th 569, 578 (6th Cir. 2021).
12. *Crosby v. University of Kentucky*, 863 F.3d 545, 552–53 (6th Cir. 2017).
13. *Parate v. Isibor*, 868 F.2d 821, 832 (6th Cir. 1989).
14. *Ryan v. Blackwell*, 979 F.3d 519, 525 (6th Cir. 2020).
15. *Cleveland Board of Education v. Loudermill*, 470 U.S. 532, 538–39 (1985).
16. *Dixon v. Alabama State Board of Education*, 294 F.2d 150, 158–59 (5th Cir. 1961).
17. *Flaim v. Med. College of Ohio*, 418 F.3d 629, 633–37 (6th Cir. 2005).
18. *Wisconsin v. Constantineau*, 400 U.S. 433, 437 (1971).
19. *Siegert v. Gilley*, 500 U.S. 226, 233 (1991).
20. *Paul v. Davis*, 424 U.S. 693, 701, 710–11 (1976).
21. *Flaim*, 418 F.3d at 633–34.
22. *Mathews v. Eldridge*, 424 U.S. 319, 334–35 (1976).
23. *Cleveland Board of Education v. Loudermill*, 470 U.S. 532, 546 (1985).

24. *Matthews*, 424 U.S. at 334–35.
25. *Doe v. Baum*, 903 F.3d 575, 581 (6th Cir. 2018).
26. *Flaim*, 418 F.3d. at 635.
27. *Id.* at 635.
28. *Nash v. Auburn University*, 812 F.2d 655, 665 (11th Cir. 1987); *Henson v. Honor Comm. of University of Virginia*, 719 F.2d 69, 73 (4th Cir. 1983).
29. *Flaim*, 418 F.3d. at 635.
30. *Riccio v. County of Fairfax*, 907 F.2d 1459, 1469 (4th Cir. 1990); *Bills v. Henderson*, 631 F.2d 1287, 1298 (6th Cir. 1980); *Winnick v. Manning*, 460 F.2d 545, 550 (2d Cir. 1972).
31. *Lassiter v. Dep't of Soc. Servs. of Durham County*, 452 U.S. 18, 25 (1981).
32. *Osteen v. Henley*, 13 F.3d 221, 225 (7th Cir. 1993); *Gorman v. University of R.I.*, 837 F.2d 7, 16 (1st Cir. 1988).
33. *Gabrilowitz v. Newman*, 582 F.2d 100, 107 (1st Cir. 1978).
34. *Flaim*, 418 F.3d at 636.
35. *Osteen*, 13 F.3d at 225.
36. *Davis v. Alaska*, 415 U.S. 308, 316 (1974).
37. *Baum*, 903 F.3d at 581.
38. *Haidak v. University of Massachusetts-Amherst*, 933 F.3d 56, 69 (1st Cir. 2019).
39. *Baum*, 903 F.3d at 581.
40. *Haidak*, 933 F.3d at 69–70.
41. *Flaim*, 418 F.3d at 642.
42. *Id.*
43. *Goss v. Lopez*, 419 U.S. 565, 580 (1975).
44. *Flaim*, 418 F.3d at 642.
45. *Yu v. Idaho State University*, 15 F.4th 1236, 1242 (9th Cir. 2021).
46. *Chapman v. California*, 386 U.S. 18, 44 (1967) (Stewart, J., concurring).

Chapter 5

The Double Security
Dual Sovereignty and State Constitutional Considerations

> In the compound republic of America, the power surrendered by the people is first divided between two distinct governments, and then the portion allotted to each subdivided among distinct and separate departments. Hence a double security arises to the rights of the people. The different governments will control each other, at the same time that each will be controlled by itself.—James Madison[1]

In a sense, the American Revolution was a dispute over whether ultimate power was vested in the British Parliament or divided between Parliament and the colonial legislatures.[2] Under the British doctrine of sovereignty, "there had to be in every state one final, supreme, indivisible, lawmaking authority. Otherwise, the government would end up with that absurdity of an imperium in imperio, a power within a power. And in the British Empire that sovereignty could be located only in Parliament."[3]

Conversely, the American view, as expressed by various statesmen and colonial assemblies, was that ultimate power was effectively divided. Parliament had ultimate power over the colonies in some areas such as trade, but the colonial legislatures had ultimate power in other areas such as local taxation taxes.[4] "The proper location of sovereignty—this supreme lawmaking power—became the issue that finally broke up the empire."[5]

By the eve of the Revolution, there was "a radically new conception of the empire. Each of the thirteen colonies, they contended, was completely independent of Parliament, but each retained an allegiance to the king as the common link in the empire."[6] In other words, power was not exclusively in the Parliament or divided between Parliament and the colonial legislatures.

Rather power was exclusively in the colonial legislatures. Other than allegiance to the King, the colonies were effectively independent, a theory of sovereignty that eventually would describe Britain's relationship with Australia, Canada, New Zealand, and other nations which retain allegiance to the Queen.[7]

Thus, in 1776, when the thirteen colonies declared their independence and severed their allegiance to the King, "the States considered themselves fully sovereign nations."[8] The Declaration of Independence speaks of "free and independent states" with the "Full Power to levy War, conclude Peace, contract Alliances, establish Commerce, and to do all other Acts and Things which Independent States may of right do."[9] The Articles of Confederation explicitly recognized that each State "retains its sovereignty, freedom, and independence, which is not by this confederation expressly delegated to the United States, in Congress assembled."[10]

Yet, the Articles of Confederation was not a "formidable central government," but "a treaty among thirteen sovereign states, an alliance that not all that different from the present-day European Union."[11] The Articles "had no real executive or judicial authority and congressional resolutions were merely recommendations left to the States to enforce."[12] It was the inability of the Confederation Congress to deal with the challenges facing *all* the States and prevent the abuses by individual state legislators that led to the Constitutional Convention of 1787.[13]

The effort to ratify the Constitution revived the pre-independence dispute over whether sovereignty could be divided.[14] If the Americans had accepted the British view and sovereignty could not be divided, then "either the new federal government would absorb all power to itself or the states would remain independent and sovereign as they were under the Articles."[15] The solution to the questions, developed by James Wilson, was to say that sovereignty was not located in the national government or the States, but in the People.[16]

This notion of the People being sovereign has profound implications.[17] First, because the People, not the legislature or the government, are sovereign, fundamental principles can "be lifted out of the lawmaking and other governmental processes and institutions of government and set above them."[18] The Constitution becomes "a fixed fundamental law superior to ordinary legislation."[19] Because "the power of the people is superior to" the government, "where the will of the [government], declared in its statutes [and executive actions], stands in opposition to that of the people, declared in the Constitution," the Constitution prevails.[20] Second, because the People are sovereign, the People may allocate portions of "their sovereign power to their different representatives and agents at both the state and national levels."[21]

In establishing the Constitution, the People "split the atom of sovereignty" and created "two orders of government, each with its own direct relationship, its own privity, its own set of mutual rights and obligations to the people who sustain it and are governed by it."[22] This division of sovereignty between the States and the National Government "is a defining feature of our Nation's constitutional blueprint."[23] The division of power between *dual sovereigns*, the States and the National Government, is reflected throughout the Constitution's text,[24] as well as its structure.[25]

"Just as the separation and independence of the coordinate branches of the Federal Government serve to prevent the accumulation of excessive power in any one branch, a healthy balance of power between the States and the Federal Government will reduce the risk of tyranny and abuse from either front."[26] Phrased differently, although the People, in the exercise of their sovereignty, granted vast power to the National Government, the National Government remains one of enumerated, hence limited, powers.[27] Indeed, "that those limits may not be mistaken, or forgotten, the constitution is written."[28]

Because "the federal balance is too essential a part of our constitutional structure and plays too vital a role in securing freedom,"[29] the Supreme Court has intervened to support the sovereign prerogatives of both the States and the National Government. In order to preserve the sovereignty of the National Government, the Court has prevented the States from imposing term limits on members of Congress,[30] and instructing members of Congress as to how to vote on certain issues.[31] Similarly, the Courts have invalidated state laws infringing on the right to travel,[32] that undermine the Nation's foreign policy,[33] and exempting a State from generally applicable regulations of interstate commerce.[34]

Conversely, "the preservation of the States, and the maintenance of their governments, are as much within the design and care of the Constitution as the preservation of the Union and the maintenance of the National Government. The Constitution, in all its provisions, looks to an indestructible Union, composed of indestructible States."[35] Recognizing that "the States retain substantial sovereign powers under our constitutional scheme, powers with which Congress does not readily interfere,"[36] and that "the erosion of state sovereignty is likely to occur a step at a time,"[37] the National Government may not compel the States to pass particular legislation,[38] to require state officials to enforce federal law,[39] to dictate the location of the State Capitol,[40] or to regulate purely local matters.[41]

While Congress can require officials at state colleges and universities to comply with specified requirements of certain things as a condition of receiving federal funds, this power is limited,[42] "Congress has no authority to order the States to regulate according to its instructions. Congress may offer the States grants and require the States to comply with accompanying conditions, but the States must have a genuine choice whether to accept the offer."[43]

The People's decision to divide sovereignty impacts public universities in three ways. First, because the People of the United States allocated a portion of their sovereignty to the States, the People of a particular State must adopt a State Constitution to establish and limit their state government. Second, because the National Government may not interfere with State functions, officials at public institutions have a federal constitutional institutional academic freedom against the National Government. Third, while public college and university officials have no *federal* constitutional institutional academic freedom against the creating State, the State Constitution and/or state law may establish a degree of *state* institutional academic freedom for these officials against the creating State.

This three-part chapter focuses on the consequences of the People's decision to divide their sovereignty between the National Government and the States. Part I discusses both the nature of the State Constitutions and how the State Constitutions may limit public universities in religion and race. Part II discusses the idea of state colleges and universities that have "institutional academic freedom" against the National Government or the State that created the college or university. Put another way, does either the United States Constitution or the State Constitution limit the power of the National Government or the State Government over a public college or university? Part III summarizes the major cases discussed in this chapter.

I. THE NATURE OF STATE CONSTITUTIONS

This part explores the nature of State Constitutions by focusing on their unique characteristics and some specific applications to public colleges and universities. It discusses how State Constitutions are limitations on power rather than grants of power, often impose affirmative obligations for the government to act, and guarantee greater liberty. This part then examines applications of the State Constitutions to public colleges and universities in the context of religious liberty and racial preferences.

A. Limitations on Power Rather than Grants of Power

The State Constitutions differ fundamentally from the United States Constitution. Instead of an all-powerful national government,[44] the national charter establishes a government of enumerated powers.[45] This means that before Congress can enact a law, Congress must be able to point to a specific provision of the Constitution authorizing it to act. While Congress' powers are broad, particularly with respect to the Commerce Clause,[46] they are not all encompassing.[47] For example, the National Government has no "authority to enact legislation for the public good," what the Supreme Court has described as a 'police power.'"[48]

Conversely, the State Constitutions have established a government of broad powers,[49] subject only to the limitations imposed by delegation of power to the National Government and the limitations set out in both the United States and State Constitutions.[50] The National Government lacks a "police power," but the States "have broad authority to enact legislation for the public good."[51]

Because State Constitutions are often amended or even completely revised, they often are more reflective of the contemporary values of society.[52] As the leader of the commission that drafted Virginia's 1971 Constitution explained, "a state constitution is a fit place for the people of a state to record their moral values, their definition of justice, their hopes for the common good. A state constitution defines a way of life."[53]

B. Affirmative Obligations to Act

To protect the liberty of the People, individually and collectively, from constitutional actors and the ever-shifting political winds,[54] the National and State Constitutions limit, with "elegant specificity,"[55] the discretion of constitutional actors to pursue a particular end by a particular means.[56] These limitations take the form of either requirements or prohibitions on constitutional actors.[57]

While Americans are familiar with the idea of constitutional provisions as prohibitions, they are less familiar with the notion of constitutional provisions that impose requirements on government to act in a particular way.[58] Yet, the fifty State Constitutions frequently require the state government to act in a particular way.[59] For example, state constitutions generally require their legislatures to establish public school systems of a particular quality.[60] Absent such a state constitutional provision, state legislatures would have absolute discretion whether to pursue the end of a statewide public school system and to choose the means of achieving this end.[61]

In a sense, these requirements are "duties"[62] and the judiciary must engage in a process-based review to determine whether the state government has violated its duty of care.[63] These "duties" are effectively explicit textual limitations on the government's discretion to act or refrain from acting. Absent a textual limitation establishing a "duty," state governments have absolute discretion to act or refrain from acting. Conversely, with the textual limitation establishing the "duty," state governments must act.[64]

C. Greater Protections of Liberty

The United States "Constitution sets a floor for the protection of individual rights. The constitutional floor is sturdy and often high, but it is a floor. Other federal, state, and local government entities generally possess authority to safeguard individual rights above and beyond the rights secured by the [United States] Constitution."[65] Although state courts often interpret state constitutional provisions in the same manner as the Supreme Court interprets national constitutional provisions,[66] "nothing compels the state court to imitate federal interpretation of the liberty and property guarantee in the U.S. Constitution when it comes to the rights found in their own constitutions, even guarantees that match the federal one's letter for letter."[67] Indeed, because the Burger Court's decisions prompted a revival of state constitutional law in the early 1970's,[68] "it would be most unwise these days not also to raise the state constitutional questions."[69]

"There often are sound reasons for interpreting the [national and state] guarantees differently."[70] First, a decision resting entirely on a state constitutional provision is insulated from review by the U.S. Supreme Court.[71] Second, a state supreme court may "allow local conditions and traditions to affect their interpretations of a constitutional guarantee and the remedies imposed to implement that guarantee."[72] Third, in areas where constitutional analysis is difficult, "it may be more to tolerate fifty-one imperfect solutions rather than to impose one imperfect solution on the country as a whole, particularly when imperfection may be something we have to live within a given area."[73] Fourth, just as state courts have been at the forefront of developing judicial doctrines in tort, contract, and property, state judges could facilitate the development of constitutional analysis at both the state and national levels.[74]

D. State Constitutional Applications to Public Universities

The possibility that a State Constitution may provide greater restrictions on the government has significant implications for public universities, particularly in the context of religious liberty and racial preferences. Both of those topics are discussed in some detail below.

1. Greater Religious Liberty

As explained in chapters 1 and 2, if a public institution has an "all comers" policy concerning membership in student organizations, *Christian Legal Society v. Martinez* allows a public institution's officials to adopt policies to force religious groups to accept members who reject fundamental tenets of the faith.

Christian Legal Society resolves the federal constitutionality of such "all-comers" policies, it does not address whether state law may preclude the forced inclusion of those who disagree with the faith. Although the issue apparently is one of national first impression, it would not be surprising if a state court determined that its State Constitution prohibited its state government from indirectly forcing an organization to admit members who disagreed with the organization's objectives. Indeed, after the U.S. Supreme Court diminished religious freedom in *Employment Division v. Smith*, various state courts held that their respective State Constitutions provided greater protection for religious freedom.[75]

Post-*Smith*, about half of the States have state Religious Freedom Restoration Acts ("RFRA").[76] Although there is some variance in scope, most state RFRA's provide "no government shall impose a substantial burden on the religious exercise" unless the burden furthers "a compelling governmental interest," and does so by "the least restrictive means."[77] To the extent that a student group's position is the result of religious belief, these state laws seem to prohibit government from indirectly forcing the inclusion of dissenters. As a practical matter, these statutes codify the legal standard prior to the Supreme Court's decision in *Smith*.[78]

Moreover, in some instances, specific state laws may protect the rights of student religious organizations to exclude nonbelievers. For example, Kentucky prohibits public institutional administrators from interfering with a student religious organization's "ordering of its internal affairs, selection of leaders and members, defining of doctrines and principles, and resolving of organizational disputes in the furtherance of its mission, or in its determination that only persons committed to its mission should conduct such activities."[79]

2. Limitations on Racial Preferences

The National Constitution allows officials at public colleges and universities to utilize racial preferences as a means of obtaining the educational benefits of a diverse student body, but the People of some States have adopted state constitutional provisions mandating an end to racial preferences.[80] In *Schutte v. Coalition to Defend Affirmative Action, Integration, & Immigrant Rights & Fight for Equality by Any Means Necessary*,[81] the Supreme Court rejected a federal constitutional challenge to such measures.[82] In sum, although higher education administrators may wish to use racial preferences, the sovereign People of the State—the ultimate owners of the state college or university—may disagree. The will of sovereign People, as expressed in their State Constitution, prevails.

II. INSTITUTIONAL ACADEMIC FREEDOM

A. Nature of Institutional Academic Freedom

Some late twentieth-century judicial decisions suggested there was an "institutional academic freedom."[83] Unlike private institutions, public colleges and universities are still subject to control by the State that created the campuses. Institutional academic freedom assumes either the United States Constitution or the State Constitution limits the power of the State Government over a public college or university.

Institutional academic freedom involves the "autonomous decision-making by the academy itself."[84] As described by Justice Frankfurter in a concurring opinion, it allows the institution to determine, without interference from outside the academy, who may teach, what may be taught, how it will be taught, and who may study.[85]

The sheer complexity of the academic task demands a degree of institutional autonomy. It is one thing for a legislature or some centralized state agency to define a university's mission, establish a program in a particular discipline, or mandate that an institution be selective in its admissions. It is something altogether different for a state government to hire faculty members, determine the best approach to teaching a specific subject, or sort through the literally thousands of applications that some institutions receive for admissions. Because educating undergraduate and graduates or pursuing academic inquiry in a variety of fields is fundamentally different from most governmental functions, public higher education requires a greater degree of flexibility and independent discretion.

While there is an obvious practical need for some form of institutional academic freedom against the creating State and while there is language in Supreme Court opinions supporting concept, "the Court has never invalidated a statute, regulation, or policy because it violates institutional academic freedom."[86] As discussed more fully below, the Supreme Court implicitly rejected the notion of a state public institution having a national constitutional institutional academic freedom against the creating State. At the same time, in some States, the State Constitution or state law may give public colleges and universities a state institutional academic freedom against the creating State.

B. No National Institutional Academic Freedom

State colleges or universities have no *national* constitutional right to institutional academic freedom against the creating State. Indeed, in those instances where the State seeks to regulate a public institution, judicial recognition of a federal constitutional right to institutional academic freedom likely undermines the principles of democratic accountability. Many, if not most, States have adopted statutes mandating that the public institutions are subject to control by the Governor and/or the state legislature.

Most obviously, the governing boards of the institution of higher education, sometimes called visitors, regents, trustees, or governors, typically are appointed by the Governor with the advice and consent of at least one legislative chamber. These provisions reinforce a basic point: a public institution belongs to the sovereign People of a State, not to the university administration, faculty, alumni, or students. If the sovereign People, through their elected representatives, want to define admissions criteria, the admissions processes, curricula, or tuition levels, then the sovereign People have that right.

The Supreme Court implicitly rejected the notion of a federal constitutional right to institutional academic freedom in *Schuette*.[87] In deciding the People of a State could amend their State Constitution to remove the ability of a state university to consider race in the admissions process, Justice Kennedy, announcing the judgment of the Court, observed: "there is no authority in the Constitution of the United States or in this Court's precedents for the Judiciary to set aside [state] laws that commit this policy determination to the voters . . . Democracy does not presume that some subjects are either too divisive or too profound for public debate."[88]

C. The State Constitution or State Law May Provide State Institutional Academic Freedom

As Justice Scalia, joined by Justice Thomas, noted in *Schutte*, each State has "near-limitless sovereignty . . . to design its governing structure as it sees fit."[89] A State may choose to create a university or close a university.[90] It may choose to allow state institutional officials to make certain decisions and then abolish or transfer that decision-making authority to others.[91] Therefore, if officials at public colleges or universities possess a state institutional academic freedom against the creating State, it is because the State Constitution or statute grants such rights.

Given the diversity of the nation, it is not surprising that the States vary widely in whether the State Constitutions provide institutional academic freedom against the creating State. Analyzing the various state constitutional provisions and the judicial decisions and attorney general opinions, one scholar suggested four distinct categories of "constitutional autonomy."[92]

First, in California, Michigan, and Minnesota, the "state courts have offered relatively well-developed standards for the overall legal framework of constitutional autonomy, and, most significantly, where cases reflect considerable judicial deference to the constitutional autonomy possessed by institutional or system governing boards."[93]

Second, in Idaho, Louisiana, Montana, Nevada, New Mexico, North Dakota, and Oklahoma,[94] there is "favorable judicial treatment of constitutional autonomy but with relatively fewer cases and, even more importantly, with a less well-developed legal framework regarding the contours of constitutional autonomy in the state."[95] "A substantially restricted form of constitutional autonomy may exist in Nebraska and South Dakota."[96]

Third, in, Florida, Georgia, and Hawaii,[97] the courts have "not clearly answered whether constitutional autonomy exists as a recognized legal doctrine by state courts."[98]

Finally, in Alabama, Alaska, Arizona, Colorado, Mississippi, Missouri, and Utah,[99] the "courts have either explicitly rejected constitutional autonomy or cast heavy doubt on the potential for its recognition by courts."[100] More specifically, "recognition by courts of constitutional autonomy in Alabama, Alaska, and Mississippi, though not completely settled, appears unlikely."[101] "For Arizona, Colorado, Missouri, and Utah, legal decisions and attorney general opinions indicate that constitutional autonomy does not enjoy judicial recognition."[102]

Of course, in some States there is no indication in the State Constitutions of any sort of constitutional autonomy for public institutions. Nevertheless, the legislature, through the enactment of statutes, may have given officials at public colleges and universities a degree of state institutional academic freedom. For example, the Supreme Court of Kentucky has determined state universities are part of the executive branch,[103] but independent of the Governor's control.[104] Unlike state constitutional provisions, a legislative provision granting autonomy can be repealed at any time. Thus, if a legislative majority is dissatisfied with how college or university officials have exercised this statutory autonomy, the legislature may modify or repeal the statute conferring the autonomy.

III. SUMMARY OF MAJOR CASES DISCUSSED IN THE CHAPTER

Christian Legal Society v. Martinez, 561 U.S. 661 (2010)

The Supreme Court held a public university may require recognized student organizations to admit "all comers" as a condition of recognition. Consequently, a student religious group was required to admit students who disagreed with its beliefs.

Employment Division, Department of Human Resources of Oregon v. Smith, 494 U.S. 872 (1990)

The Supreme Court modified the standard for determining if there was a violation of the Free Exercise Clause. If there is a religiously neutral statute of general applicability, there is no requirement for government to grant a religious exemption. Accordingly, the Court upheld the dismissal of drug counselors who ingested peyote as part of a sacramental ritual in the Native American Church. The decision prompted Congress to pass the Religious Freedom Restoration Act. Several States have enacted similar laws.

Hosanna-Tabor Evangelical Lutheran Church and School v. EEOC, 565 U.S. 171 (2012)

The Supreme Court decided the First Amendment Religious Clause contained a ministerial exception, which guarantees a large degree of autonomy to religious organizations. As a result, rejecting the age discrimination claim of a teacher in a faith-based school could not pursue an age discrimination claim.

National Federation of Independent Business v. Sebelius, 567 U.S. 519 (2012)

The Supreme Court invalidated some provisions of the Patient Protection and Affordable Care Act including a provision requiring the States to expand Medicaid or lose all Medicaid funds. The case is significant for establishing limits on Congress' ability to require certain behaviors as a condition of receiving federal funds. While Congress can impose conditions of the receipt of future funds, it cannot require the forfeiture of existing funds.

Rumsfeld v. Forum for Academic & Institutional Rights, 547 U.S. 47 (2006)

The Supreme Court determined the federal government could require colleges and universities which receive federal funds to allow military recruiters on campus. The case is significant for the ability to force institutions to compromise academic freedom as a condition of receiving federal funds.

Schutte v. Coalition to Defend Affirmative Action, Integration, & Immigrant Rights & Fight for Equality by Any Means Necessary, 572 U.S 291 (2014)

The Supreme Court decided the People of a State could amend their State Constitution to ban the consideration of public education, employment, and contracting. The case is significant as it implicitly rejects the idea of a federal constitutional right of academic freedom against the State that creates the state university.

Sweezy v. New Hampshire, 354 U.S. 234 (1957)

The Supreme Court concluded state university officials could not punish a speaker on a university campus for refusing to answer questions about whether he was engaged in subversive activities because the inquiries violated his rights to academic freedom and political expression. The case is significant for its discussion of the importance of both individual and institutional academic freedom.

NOTES

1. The Federalist No. 51 (James Madison).
2. Gordon S. Wood, Power and Liberty: Constitutionalism in the American Revolution 18–26, (2021).
3. *Id.* at 21.
4. *Id.* at 22–25.
5. *Id.* at 19.
6. *Id.* at 25.
7. *Id.* at 26.
8. *Franchise Tax Board of California v. Hyatt*, 139 S. Ct. 1485, 1493 (2019).
9. Declaration of Independence.
10. Articles of Confederation, art. II.
11. Wood, *supra* note 2, at 55.
12. *Id.* at 55.

13. Michael Stokes Paulsen & Luke Paulsen, THE CONSTITUTION: AN INTRODUCTION 9–10 (2015).

14. Wood, *supra* note 2, at 92–95.

15. *Id.* at 93.

16. *Id.* at 93–94.

17. *Id.* at 95.

18. *Id.* at 46.

19. *Id.* at 49.

20. THE FEDERALIST No. 78 (Alexander Hamilton).

21. Wood, *supra* note 2 at 95.

22. *U.S. Term Limits v. Thornton*, 514 U.S.779, 838 (1995) (Kennedy, J., concurring).

23. *Federal Maritime Commission v. South Carolina State Ports Authority*, 535 U.S. 743, 751 (2002).

24. *Printz, v. United States*, 521 U.S. 898, 919 (1997).

25. *Alde v. Maine*, 527 U.S. 706, 714–15 (1999).

26. *Gregory v. Ashcroft*, 501 U.S. 452, 458 (1991).

27. *McCulloch v. Maryland*, 17 U.S. (4 Wheat.) 316, 405 (1819).

28. *Marbury v. Madison*, 5 U.S. (1 Cranch) 137, 176 (1803).

29. *United States v. Lopez*, 514 U.S. 549, 578 (1995) (Kennedy, J., joined by O'Connor, J., concurring).

30. *U.S. Term Limits*, 514 U.S. at 800–801.

31. *Cook v. Gralike*, 531 U.S. 510, 519–22 (2001).

32. *Saenz v. Roe*, 526 U.S. 489 (1999).

33. *Crosby v. National Foreign Trade Council*, 530 U.S. 363, 372–74 (2000).

34. *Reno v. Condon*, 528 U.S. 141, 150 (2000).

35. *Texas v. White*, 74 U.S. (7 Wall.) 700, 725 (1868).

36. *Gregory*, 501 U.S. at 461.

37. *South Carolina v. Baker*, 485 U.S. 505, 533 (1988) (O'Connor, J., dissenting).

38. *New York v. United States*, 505 U.S. 144, 162 (1992).

39. *Printz*, 521 U.S. at 935.

40. *Coyle v. Smith*, 221 U.S. 559, 579 (1911).

41. *United States v. Morrison*, 529 U.S. 598, 617–19 (2000); *Lopez*, 514 U.S. at 561 n.3.

42. *Rumsfeld v. Forum for Academic & Institutional Rights*, 547 U.S. 47, 69–70 (2006).

43. *National Federation of Independent Businesses v. Sebelius*, 567 U.S. 519, 588 (2012).

44. *McCulloch v. Maryland*, 17 U.S. (4 Wheat.) 316, 405 (1819).

45. *Morrison*, 529 U.S. at 607.

46. U.S. Const. Art. I, § 8, cl. 3.

47. *Lopez*, 514 U.S. at 584 (Thomas, J., concurring).

48. *Bond v. United States*, 572 U.S. 844, 854 (2014).

49. *Hornbeck v. Somerset County Board of Education*, 458 A.2d 758, 785 (Md. 1983); *Board of Education v. Nyquist*, 439 N.E.2d 359, 366 n. 5 (N.Y. 1982).

50. *Almond v. Rhode Island Lottery Commission*, 756 A.2d 186, 196 (R.I. 2000).

51. *Bond*, 572 U.S. at 854.

52. *See* Robert F. Utter, *Freedom and Diversity in a Federal System: Perspectives on State Constitutions and the Washington Declaration of Rights* in DEVELOPMENTS IN STATE CONSTITUTIONAL LAW 239, 241–42 (Bradley McGraw, ed. 1984).

53. A.E. Dick Howard, *The Renaissance of State Constitutional Law*, 1 EMERGING ISSUES IN STATE CONSTITUTIONAL LAW 1, 14 (1988).

54. *See* Randy Barnett, OUR REPUBLICAN CONSTITUTION: SECURING THE LIBERTY & SOVEREIGNTY OF WE THE PEOPLE (2016).

55. *Arizona State Legislature v. Arizona Indep. Redistrict Commission*, 135 S. Ct. 2652, 2690 (2015) (Roberts, C.J, joined by Scalia, Thomas, & Alito, JJ., dissenting).

56. *Patel v. Texas Department of Licensing & Regulation*, 469 S.W.3d 69, 92 (Tex. 2015) (Willett, J., joined by Lehman & Devine, JJ., concurring).

57. William E. Thro, *No Clash of Constitutional Values: Respecting Freedom & Equality in Public University Sexual Assault Cases*, 28 REGENT UNIV. L. REV. 197 (2016).

58. Abner S. Greene, *What Is Constitutional Obligation?* 93 B.U.L. REV. 1239, 1241–42 (2013).

59. Emily Zackin, LOOKING FOR RIGHTS IN ALL THE WRONG PLACES: WHY STATE CONSTITUTIONS CONTAIN AMERICA'S POSITIVE RIGHTS 36–47 (2013).

60. William E. Thro, *Judicial Humility: The Enduring Legacy of Rose v. Council for Better Education*, 98 KY. L.J. 717, 725–26 (2010).

61. Scott R. Bauries, *State Constitutions and Individual Rights: Conceptual Convergence in School Finance Litigation*, 18 GEO. MASON L. REV. 301, 358–59 (2011).

62. Scott R. Bauries, *The Education Duty*, 47 WAKE FOREST L. REV. 705, 747–48 (2012).

63. Scott R. Bauries, *Perversity as Rationality in Teacher Evaluation*, 72 ARK. L. REV. 325, 358 (2019).

64. Helen Hershkoff, *Positive Rights and State Constitutions: The Limits of Federal Rationality Review*, 112 HARV. L. REV. 1131, 1137 (1999).

65. *American Legion v. American Humanist Association*, 139 S. Ct. 2067, 2094 (2019).

66. *Virginia College Building Authority v. Lynn*, 538 S.E.2d 682, 691 (Va. 2000) (Virginia courts have "always been informed by the United States Supreme Court Establishment Clause jurisprudence in [construing] Article I, § 16").

67. Jeffery Sutton, 51 IMPERFECT SOLUTIONS: STATES AND THE MAKING OF AMERICAN CONSTITUTIONAL LAW 16 (2018).

68. *See* A.E. Dick Howard, *State Courts and Constitutional Rights in the Day of the Burger Court*, 62 VA. L. REV. 873 (1976).

69. William J. Brennan, *State Constitutions and the Protection of Individual Rights*, 90 HARV. L. REV. 489, 502 (1977).

70. Sutton, *supra* note 67, at 16.

71. *Michigan v. Long*, 463 U.S. 1032 (1983).

72. Sutton, *supra* note 67, at 17.

73. *Id.* at 19.

74. *Id.* at 20.

75. Douglas Laycock, *Theology Scholarships, The Pledge of Allegiance, And Religious Liberty: Avoiding the Extremes*, 118 HARV. L. REV. 155, 211–12 (2004) (discussing cases).

76. *See* Ala. Const. art. I, § 3.01; Ariz. Rev. Stat. § 41–1493.01; Ark Code 16–123–401; Conn. Gen. Stat. § 52–571b; Fla. Stat. § 767.01; Idaho Code § 73–402; Ill. Rev. Stat. Ch. 775, § 35/1; Ind. Code 34–13–9–5; Kan. Stat. §60–5301, et seq.; Ky. Rev. Stat. §446.350; La. Rev. Stat. §13:5231, et seq.; Miss. Code §11–61–1 Mo. Rev. Stat. §1.302; N.M. Stat. §28–22–1, et seq.; Okla. Stat. tit. 51, §251, et seq. Pa. Stat. tit. 71, §2403; R.I. Gen. Laws §42–80.1–1, et seq.; S.C. Code §1–32–10, et seq.; Tenn. Code §4–1–407; Tex. Civ. Prac. & Remedies Code §110.001, et seq; Va. Code §57–1, et seq.

77. *See* Christopher C. Lund, *Religious Freedom After Gonzales*, 55 S.D. LAW REVIEW 467, 476 (2011); James W. Wright, Jr., Note, *Making State Religious Freedom Restoration Amendments Effective*, 61 ALABAMA LAW REVIEW 425, 426 (2010).

78. *Sherbert v. Verner*, 374 U.S. 398 (1963).

79. Ky. Rev. Stat. 164.348(2)(h).

80. The People of Arizona, California, Florida, Michigan, Nebraska, New Hampshire, Oklahoma, and Washington have amended their State Constitutions to ban racial preferences in university admissions. *See* Ariz. Const. art. 1, § 36; Cal. Const. art. 1, § 31; Fla. Const. art. 1, § 2; Mich. Const. art. 1, § 26; Neb. Const. art. I, § 30; N.H. Const. part 1, art. 2.; Okla. Const. art. 2, § 36A; and Wash. Const. art. 9, § 1.

81. *Schutte v. Coalition to Defend Affirmative Action, Integration, & Immigrant Rights & Fight for Equality by Any Means Necessary*, 572 U.S 291 (2014).

82. *Id.* at 312–13 (Kennedy, J., joined by Roberts, C.J. & Alito, J., announcing the judgment of the Court).

83. William A. Kaplin, Barbara A. Lee, Neal H. Hutchens, & Jacob H. Rooksby, THE LAW OF HIGHER EDUCATION 775–79 (6th ed. 2020).

84. *Regents of the University of Michigan v. Ewing*, 474 U.S. 214, 226 n. 12 (1985).

85. *Sweezy v. New Hampshire*, 354 U.S. 234, 263 (1957) (Frankfurter, J. concurring).

86. *Urofsky v. Gilmore*, 216 F.3d 401, 411–12 (4th Cir. 2000) (en banc).

87. *Schutte*, 572 U.S. at 314.

88. *Id.* at 314 (Kennedy, J., joined by Roberts, C.J., and Alito, J., announcing the judgment of the Court).

89. *Id.* at 327 (Scalia, J., joined by Thomas, J., concurring).

90. *Id.* at 328 (Scalia, J., joined by Thomas, J., concurring).

91. *Id.* at 335–36 (Breyer, J., concurring).

92. Neal H. Hutchens, *Preserving the Independence of Public Higher Education: An Examination of State Constitutional Autonomy Provisions for Public Colleges and Universities*, 35 J.C. & U.L. 271, 281 (2009).

93. *Id.* at 281–82.

94. *Id.* at 311.

95. *Id.* at 281.

96. *Id.* at 311.

97. *Id.* at 311.
98. *Id.* at 282.
99. *Id.* at 311.
100. *Id.* at 282.
101. *Id.* at 311.
102. *Id.*
103. *University of Kentucky v. Moore*, 599 S.W.3d 798 (2019).
104. *Beshear ex rel. Kentucky v. Bevin ex rel. Kentucky*, 498 S.W.3d 355 (Ky. 2016).

Chapter 6

The Will of the People, Not Their Agents

Judicial Enforcement of Federal Law and Immunity

The interpretation of the laws is the proper and peculiar province of the courts. A constitution is, in fact, and must be regarded by the judges as, a fundamental law. It therefore belongs to them to ascertain its meaning as well as the meaning of any particular act proceeding from the legislative body. If there should happen to be an irreconcilable variance between the two, that which has the superior obligation and validity ought, of course, to be preferred; or, in other words, the Constitution ought to be preferred to the statute, the intention of the people to the intention of their agents.

Nor does this conclusion by any means suppose a superiority of the judicial to the legislative power. It only supposes that the power of the people is superior to both, and that where the will of the legislature, declared in its statutes, stands in opposition to that of the people, declared in the Constitution, the judges ought to be governed by the latter rather than the former. They ought to regulate their decisions by the fundamental laws rather than by those which are not fundamental.—Alexander Hamilton[1]

Hamilton's words, written to persuade the People of New York to ratify the Constitution, reflect America's unique arrangement concerning sovereignty—the final, supreme, indivisible lawmaking authority.[2] The People—not the Queen or the Parliament or the Party or the Faith—are sovereign.[3] The People, in the exercise of their sovereignty, have created a written Constitution—"a fixed fundamental law superior to ordinary [legislative or executive actions]."[4] Because the Constitution reflects the Will of the sovereign People, the Constitution is effectively sovereign.[5]

Public officials—whether elected, appointed, or simply a person empowered to act under the color of law—are the Agents of the People. Their actions must conform to the Will of the People as expressed in the Constitution. Were it otherwise, then the Will of the People's Agents—the actions of public officials—would be greater than the Will of the People—the words of the Nation's fundamental law.

Hamilton's words also foreshadowed America's practice of judicial review of the actions of public officials and judicial enforcement of the constitutional limitations. The Constitution, which prohibits the government officials from taking certain actions and requires them to take specific actions, is the supreme law of the land.[6] Indeed, the federal government's powers "are defined and limited; and that those limits may not be mistaken, or forgotten, the constitution is written."[7]

When the Supreme Court addresses constitutional issues, the resulting interpretations of the Constitution are "the supreme law of the land"[8] even though the other branches or the States may interpret the Constitution differently.[9] Once the Supreme Court renders a decision, constitutional actors must "follow the Court's interpretations, not just in the particular case announcing those interpretations, but in similar cases as well."[10] While the legislative and executive actors can choose how to remedy the constitutional violations,[11] "the government can and does lose in its own courts and then respect those judgements."[12]

These same principles apply to officials at public colleges and universities. Because constitutional commands often are ambiguous and because public institutional officials are human beings, there will be circumstances when students, faculty, and/or staff allege a violation of the Constitution and/or federal law. In doing so, the plaintiffs may seek injunctions to stop the officials from violating the Constitution and/or federal law as well as damages against the public institution and individual administrators.

Although all public colleges and universities are constrained by the Constitution, not all public campuses are considered the State for purposes of sovereign immunity.[13] Some public institutions are considered parts of local government and do not have sovereign immunity.[14]

If public colleges or universities are considered the State for purposes of sovereign immunity, then litigation against these public institutions and their officials have additional levels of complexity. The courts generally can stop ongoing violations of the Constitution and federal law, but the ability of the plaintiffs to recover damages from either the public institution or individual officials turns on whether some form of immunity protects the state institution and/or individual officials.

Against this background, this four-part chapter examines judicial enforcement of the Constitution and the various immunity doctrines. Part I explains the *Ex Parte Young* doctrine, which generally allows federal courts to stop state officials, including state college and university administrators, from ongoing violations of the Constitution or federal law. Part II discusses the sovereign immunity for claims against state colleges or universities themselves. Part III discusses claims against individual state college and university administrators. Part IV summarizes the major cases discussed in this chapter.

I. THE EX PARTE YOUNG DOCTRINE

A. Overview of the Doctrine

Under the doctrine of *Ex Parte Young*,[15] federals court may hear claims against individual state officers, such as the president of a state college or university, that seek (1) a declaratory judgment that the state officer is currently violating federal law; and (2) an injunction forcing the state officials to conform their current conduct to federal law.[16] The *Ex Parte Young* doctrine is limited to suits against individual state officials seeking injunctive relief. It does not apply to suits against the State or state entities including a state college or university. Therefore, most constitutional challenges to the policies of public institutions name an official, such as the president, rather than the institution itself.

Thus, if officials of state institutions are violating the Constitution or federal law, then the *Ex Parte Young* doctrine allows federal courts to issue an injunction against an individual public institution administrator to stop the violation. However, it is important to note that this exception applies only where there is an *ongoing* violation of federal law that can be cured by declaratory or injunctive relief.[17] This exception does not apply when the alleged violation of the Constitution or federal law occurred entirely in the past.[18] In essence, someone must be violating the Constitution or federal law when the federal court makes its decision and it must be possible to stop the violation by issuing an injunction.

Because any "ruling of unconstitutionality frustrates the intent of the elected representatives of the people,"[19] the judiciary cannot force the legislative and executive actors to choose particular courses when other options are equally constitutional.[20] As such, if the judiciary determines there has been a constitutional violation, its "remedial powers . . . must be adequate to the task,"[21] but legislative and executive officials have "primary responsibility for elucidating, assessing, and solving" the problems of constitutional compliance.[22]

B. Limitations on the Doctrine

The *Ex Parte Young* doctrine is the Supreme Court's way of ensuring that "the doctrine of sovereign immunity remains meaningful, while also giving recognition to the need to prevent violations of federal law."[23] Yet, the Court also has recognized that "[t]he real interests served by [sovereign immunity] are not to be sacrificed to elementary mechanics of captions and pleading. Application of the *Young* exception must reflect a proper understanding of its role in our federal system and respect for state courts instead of a reflexive reliance on an obvious fiction."[24] Stated differently in some circumstances, the *Ex Parte Young* doctrine will not apply even though a state official is engaged in a clear violation of federal law.

The Supreme Court has imposed two significant limitations on the *Ex Parte Young* doctrine.[25] First, in *Seminole Tribe v. Florida*, the Court determined the *Ex Parte Young* doctrine was inapplicable in those situations where Congress had enacted a "comprehensive remedial scheme."[26] Put differently, if Congress already has a system in place whereby federal agencies can penalize the States for violations of federal law and take steps to prevent future violations of federal law, there is no need for the federal courts to use the *Ex Parte Young* doctrine to accomplish the same objective. While the Court has yet to define further what is meant by a "comprehensive remedial scheme," the existence of a complex administrative system to enforce Title VI, Title IX, the Rehabilitation Act, and/or other statutes suggests that officials at state institutions may be able to use this exception to avoid many different suits.

Second, and potentially more significantly, in *Idaho v Coeur d'Alene Tribe*,[27] the Court ruled that the *Ex Parte Young* doctrine was inapplicable when there were "special sovereignty interests" involved.[28] More specifically, when Idaho officials were violating federal law, an injunction to stop them essentially would have transferred the land from the State to a tribe of Native Americans.[29] The Court declared the State's interest in maintaining effective ownership of the land was greater than the need to stop an ongoing violation of federal law.[30] While the Court has not defined "special sovereignty interests," this exception could be potentially useful for state universities in the future.

II. ACTIONS AGAINST STATE COLLEGES AND UNIVERSITIES

The Eleventh Amendment provides, "the judicial power of the United States shall not be construed to extend to any suit in law or equity commenced against one of the United States by Citizens of another State or by

Citizens or Subjects of any foreign State,"[31] but "the sovereign immunity of the States neither derives from, nor is limited by, the terms of the Eleventh Amendment."[32] Indeed, the Supreme "Court has repeatedly held that the sovereign immunity enjoyed by the States extends beyond the literal text of the Eleventh Amendment."[33]

Essentially, "sovereign immunity of the States" means that private individuals or corporations cannot sue the States. Although "[e]ach situation must be addressed individually because the states have adopted different schemes, both intra and interstate, in constituting institutions of higher education,"[34] the courts have, almost without exception, agreed state colleges and universities are considered the State for purposes of sovereign immunity.[35] If state colleges or universities are considered "arms of the State," then both the entities and the administrators, when sued in their official capacities, generally have sovereign immunity from all aspects of litigation.[36]

At the same time, sovereign immunity does not mean officials of state institutions of higher education may violate law, the law is inapplicable to state colleges and universities, or the federal government could not enforce federal law against the state institution. Rather, the Supreme Court simply decided sovereign immunity prevents private parties from pursuing certain claims.

The remainder of this part has three sections. The first section supplies a general background of both the constitutional theory and the Supreme Court's sovereign immunity jurisprudence. The second section discusses the exceptions to sovereign immunity—the congressional power to "abrogate," that is to abolish or nullify and the States' powers to voluntarily waive sovereign immunity. The third section discusses sovereign immunity in state court and in the courts of another State.

A. Overview of Sovereign Immunity

"An integral component of that 'residuary and inviolable sovereignty' retained by the States is their immunity from private suits."[37] The adoption of the Constitution "did not disturb States' immunity from private suits, thus firmly enshrining this principle in our constitutional framework."[38] Indeed, "leading advocates of the Constitution assured the people in no uncertain terms that the Constitution would not strip the States of sovereign immunity."[39]

Addressing sovereign immunity specifically, Hamilton observed, "[i]t is inherent in the nature of sovereignty not to be amenable to the suit of an individual *without its consent.*"[40] Madison recognized the Constitution "leaves to the several States a residuary and inviolable sovereignty over all other objects."[41] While the States surrendered some aspects of their sovereign immunity by ratifying the Constitution, the States retained most aspects.[42]

The widespread acceptance of this proposition is demonstrated by the reaction to *Chisholm v. Georgia*,[43] where the Supreme Court ruled private citizens from one State could sue another State.[44] Almost immediately, Congress passed, and the States subsequently ratified the Eleventh Amendment, effectively overturning *Chisholm*.[45] Subsequently, the Court has explicitly acknowledged that its decision in *Chisholm* was wrong.[46]

While the text of the Eleventh Amendment is limited to "the specific provisions of the Constitution that had raised concerns during the ratification debates and formed the basis of the *Chisholm* decision,"[47] the Eleventh Amendment confirms a much broader proposition, namely the States are immune from suit.[48] "The Amendment is rooted in a recognition that the States, although a union, maintain certain attributes of sovereignty, including sovereign immunity."[49] The Supreme Court has "understood the Eleventh Amendment to stand not so much for what it says, but for the presupposition of our constitutional structure which it confirms."[50]

Sovereign immunity does not exist solely to "preven[t] federal-court judgments that must be paid out of a State's treasury,"[51] but allows the States to avoid "the indignity of subjecting a State to the coercive process of judicial tribunals at the instance of private parties."[52] "Although the sovereign immunity of the States derives at least in part from the common-law tradition, the structure and history of the Constitution make clear that the immunity exists today by constitutional design."[53]

The immunity confirmed by the Eleventh Amendment bars suits against the States by Indian Tribes,[54] foreign nations,[55] and corporations created by the National Government.[56] Moreover, it applies to proceedings in state court,[57] federal administrative proceedings,[58] admiralty,[59] and in situations where the State's treasury is not implicated.[60] In fact, there is a presumption "that the Constitution was not intended to 'rais[e] up' any proceedings against the States that were 'anomalous and unheard of when the Constitution was adopted.'"[61]

While the States have always had sovereign immunity, there was a period when the Supreme Court created so many exceptions that it effectively nullified this doctrine. In 1976, the Court determined Congress could abolish the State sovereign immunity by exercising its powers to enforce the Fourteenth Amendment.[62] In 1989, the Court extended this holding, declaring Congress could use *any* of its powers to limit the State sovereign immunity,[63] thereby giving it virtually unlimited power to strip the States of this protection.[64] Not surprisingly, Congress took advantage of these rulings and proceeded to cancel the States' sovereign immunity for most federal statutes.[65]

This all changed in 1996, in *Seminole Tribe*, when the Court reversed itself, declaring Congress' power to abrogate sovereign immunity was limited to its efforts to enforce the Fourteenth Amendment.[66] Although this ruling was constitutionally significant in that it technically limited congressional power to nullify sovereign immunity, it had little practical effect. At the time, Congress' powers to enforce the Fourteenth Amendment were almost unlimited.[67] Thus, Congress could still abrogate sovereign immunity for most federal statutes.

Nevertheless, one year later, in *City of Boerne v. Flores*,[68] the Court imposed significant limitations on the power of Congress to enforce the Fourteenth Amendment. *Flores* holds Congress' powers under Section 5 of the Fourteenth Amendment limited to enforcing the actual substantive guarantees of the Fourteenth Amendment, which include Equal Protection of the laws, the Privileges or Immunities of national citizenship, and Due Process. For legislation to be a valid exercise of congressional power to enforce the Fourteenth Amendment, Congress must make specific findings that the States have violated the Constitution. Even if those findings exist, the resulting legislation to enforce the Fourteenth Amendment must be a "proportionate response" to the violations.

Combining *Flores* and *Seminole Tribe*, congressional abrogation of sovereign immunity becomes extremely difficult. To enact a valid abrogation, Congress must first make a specific finding that the States are violating the substantive guarantees of the Constitution. Once there are such findings, Congress must then prove that abrogation of sovereign immunity for a class of claims is a proportionate response to the violations.

Supreme Court decisions illustrate this point. For example, in *Florida Prepaid*, the Court held that Congress could not abrogate sovereign immunity for intellectual property claims. In *Kimel v. Florida Board of Regents*, the Court held Congress could not abrogate sovereign immunity for Age Discrimination in Employment Act claims.[69] In *Board of Trustees of University of Alabama v. Garrett*, the Court found Congress could not abrogate sovereign immunity for employment claims under the Americans with Disabilities Act.[70] In *Federal Maritime Commission v. South Carolina State Ports Authority*, the Court ruled sovereign immunity extended to not only judicial proceedings, but also to federal administrative proceedings.[71] The Court also determined Congress did not validly abrogate states' sovereign immunity from suits for money damages in enacting the Family and Medical Leave Act's self-care provision.[72] Most recently, the Court concluded neither the Intellectual Property nor the Fourteenth Amendment authorized Congress to abrogate sovereign immunity for copyright claims.[73]

Nevertheless, during the first decade of this century, the Supreme Court upheld congressional abrogation in some contexts. In 2003, in *Hibbs*, the Court concluded sovereign immunity had been abrogated for family care provisions of the Family and Medical Leave Act.[74] In 2004, in *Tennessee Student Assistance Corp. v. Hood*, the Court found abrogation of sovereign immunity an action to discharge a student loan in bankruptcy.[75] That same year, in *Tennessee v. Lane*, the Court ruled sovereign immunity had been abrogated for claims under Title II of the Americans with Disabilities Act that involved the fundamental constitutional right of access to the Courts.[76] In *United States v. Georgia*,[77] the Court unanimously held Congress could abrogate sovereign immunity for a claim under Title I of the Americans with Disabilities Act that *was also a constitutional claim*.[78]

B. The Exceptions to Sovereign Immunity in Federal Court

1. Abrogation by Congress

Simply put, the ability of Congress to abrogate sovereign immunity depends on the constitutional power that Congress purports to use.[79] "Congress' powers under Article I of the Constitution do not include the power to subject States to suit at the hands of private individuals."[80] "Section 5 of the Fourteenth Amendment, however, does grant Congress the authority to abrogate the States' sovereign immunity."[81] This distinction between the Article I powers and the Fourteenth Amendment enforcement powers stems from the fundamentally different purposes of these two constitutional provisions.

The Article I powers define and limit the National Government to preserve the sovereignty of the States.[82] Indeed, "the Tenth Amendment confirms that the power of the Federal Government is subject to limits that may, in a given instance, reserve power to the States."[83] "The Eleventh Amendment restricts the judicial power under Article III, and Article I cannot be used to circumvent the constitutional limitations placed upon federal jurisdiction."[84] Because the Tenth and Eleventh Amendments confirm the limited nature of the Article I powers, "Congress lacks power under Article I to abrogate the States' sovereign immunity."[85] "Even when the Constitution vests in Congress complete lawmaking authority over a particular area, the Eleventh Amendment prevents congressional authorization of suits by private parties against unconsenting States."[86]

In contrast, the Fourteenth Amendment diminishes the States' sovereign authority while enhancing the power of the National Government.[87] First, both the Equal Protection Clause and the Privileges or Immunities Clause impose substantive restrictions on the States.[88] Although the Bill of Rights originally did not apply to the States,[89] the Due Process Clause incorporates most of the provisions of the Bill of Rights.[90] Second, Section 5 of the Fourteenth Amendment gives Congress the authority to enact legislation that enforces the substantive guarantees of the Fourteenth Amendment against the States.[91] Consequently, if the States have engaged in conduct that violates the

Fourteenth Amendment, then Congress can take remedial action to correct the violations and prevent future violations.[92]

Because "the Eleventh Amendment, and the principle of state sovereignty which it embodies, are necessarily limited by the enforcement provisions of § 5 of the Fourteenth Amendment,"[93] one way of enforcing the Fourteenth Amendment is to abrogate the States' sovereign immunity.[94] Put another way, if Congress is enforcing the Fourteenth Amendment, then it may abrogate the States' sovereign immunity.[95] The abrogation of sovereign immunity is an appropriate response to unconstitutional conduct by the States.

In *Seminole Tribe,* the Supreme Court reaffirmed the basic principle that Congress, acting pursuant to Section 5 of the Fourteenth Amendment, may enact legislation that abrogates constitutional sovereign immunity for claims based on a particular statute.[96] However, because the power to nullify constitutional sovereign immunity is so extraordinary, in order to do so Congress must: (1) unequivocally express its intent to abrogate in the text of the statute, and (2) act pursuant to § 5 of the Fourteenth Amendment.[97] Unless Congress satisfies both conditions, the attempt to abrogate the States' sovereign immunity is invalid.[98] Because it is relatively easy for Congress to satisfy the first condition, most of the litigation inevitably focus on the second condition.[99] Consequently the question as to whether Congress acted pursuant to Section 5 of the Fourteenth Amendment requires application of the "congruence and proportionality" test set forth in *Flores*. This test involves three questions.[100]

First, under *Flores,* the Court must "[i]dentify with some precision the scope of the constitutional right at issue."[101] This involves not only articulating the right, but also determining whether those right in questions warrants heightened scrutiny. That is, a court must consider whether the claim before it involves a fundamental right, or a suspect or quasi-suspect classification. If the right warrants heightened scrutiny, then it is easier for Congress to show a pattern of constitutional violations by the States.[102] Conversely, if the right does not call for heightened scrutiny, the standard for abrogation still is high.[103]

Second, after identifying the right at issue, a reviewing court must determine "whether Congress identified a history and pattern of unconstitutional . . . discrimination by the States."[104] Although the inquiry seems straightforward, the Supreme Court's opinions are ambiguous and uncertain regarding the significance of legislative history, the exact definition of a constitutional violation, and the number of constitutional violations necessary to establish a pattern. If there is no pattern of constitutional violations by the States, then Congress has not acted properly and the inquiry ends.[105] In such a situation, Congress has not abrogated sovereign immunity.

Third, if Congress has met the requirement of establishing a pattern of constitutional violations by the States. The Supreme Court must determine whether Congress' response is proportionate to the finding of constitutional violations.[106] Although any judgment concerning proportionality is vague and somewhat amorphous, the Court has compounded the confusion by rendering inconsistent pronouncements on how the test is applied.

B. Waivers by the States

Second, States, in the exercise of their sovereignty,[107] may voluntarily waive sovereign immunity.[108] These waivers can take four different forms.

1. Express Waivers by the States

Courts will find waivers of sovereign immunity "only where stated 'by the most expressive language or by such overwhelming implications from the text as [will] leave no room for any other reasonable construction.'"[109] Thus, States do not consent to suit in federal court merely by consenting to suit in the courts of its own creation,[110] or merely by stating their intention to "sue and be sued,"[111] or even by authorizing suits against the States "in any court of competent jurisdiction."[112] "Although a State's general waiver of sovereign immunity may subject it to suit in state court, it is not enough to waive the immunity guaranteed by the Eleventh Amendment . . . [absent] intent to subject itself to suit in federal court."[113]

Significantly, there are no constructive waivers of sovereign immunity.[114] Thus, the mere receipt of federal funds, general participation in a federal program, or an agreement to recognize and abide by federal laws, regulations, and guidelines alone are insufficient to waive sovereign immunity.[115]

2. Congress Requiring Waivers as a Condition of Receiving Federal Funds

Because "the power of Congress to authorize expenditure of public moneys for public purposes is not limited by the direct grants of legislative power found in the Constitution"[116] "objectives not thought to be within Article I's 'enumerated legislative fields' . . . may nevertheless be attained through the use of the spending power and the conditional grant of federal funds."[117] The Spending Clause[118] then is "limited only by Congress' notion of the general welfare [and] the reality, given the vast financial resources of the Federal Government, is that the Spending Clause gives 'power to the Congress to tear down the barriers, to invade the states' jurisdiction, and to become a parliament of the whole people, subject to no restrictions save such as are self-imposed.'"[119]

As a result, Congress has "a seemingly easy end run around any restrictions the Constitution might be found to impose on its ability to regulate the states. Congress need merely attach its otherwise unconstitutional regulations to any one of the large sums of federal money."[120] Because there is a federal statute requiring States to waive sovereign immunity for specified discrimination claims as a condition of receiving federal funds,[121] many federal courts declared state universities had waived sovereign immunity.[122]

Yet, there is a limit on congressional power to use the Spending Clause to exact waivers of sovereign immunity. Conditions on the use of federal funds must "govern the use of the funds."[123] If the conditions "take the form of threats to terminate other significant independent grants, the conditions are properly viewed as a means of pressuring the States to accept policy changes."[124] In such instances, the conditions are unconstitutional.[125]

3. Waivers through Litigation Conduct

When a state college or university initiates litigation in its own name, that action partially diminishes the institution's sovereign immunity by exposing the institution to the equivalent of a compulsory counterclaim that does not exceed in amount or differ in kind from the relief sought by the state college or university.[126] On occasion, some courts, including the Supreme Court, have described the initiation of litigation as constituting a "wavier" of sovereign immunity.[127]

Yet, the use of the term "waiver" is something of a mischaracterization. Sovereign immunity is immunity from suit by another party. As such, it does not actually come into play when the State or a state college or university is the plaintiff. To the contrary, there is the use of a separate power—the voluntary right of a State to invoke its right of access to a federal court to protect the States' legal interests.[128]

The Supreme Court' has implicitly recognized the resulting partial waiver encompasses only the equivalent of a compulsory counterclaim that does not exceed in amount or differ in kind from the relief sought by the States. For example, when a constitutional sovereign, such as a State, a Native American Tribe, or the National Government, initiates a suit for injunctive relief, a counterclaim or cross-claim for damages is barred.[129] In other words, filing a claim does not create a broad waiver;[130] it merely allows the adjudication of *that* claim.[131] Consequently, when a state college or university brings an action for damages in the name of the state college or university, sovereign immunity bars any counterclaim seeking damages for any amount greater than what originally was sought by the state college or university sovereign, even with respect to mandatory counterclaims.[132]

4. Removal to Federal Court Does Not Waive Immunity

Officials at state colleges and universities cannot enhance the institution's sovereign immunity by removing an action from state court to federal court,[133] but the voluntary removal of a private suit to federal court does not by itself waive the State's general immunity from such suits.[134] As the Second Circuit explained, "where a state defendant has not waived its underlying state sovereign immunity, i.e., where it is arguably protected from private suit in its own courts as well as in federal courts, the state may avail itself of removal to the federal court without sacrificing this immunity."[135]

C. Sovereign Immunity in State Court for State Law Claims

The discussion above applies to both state and federal claims against state colleges and universities brought in *federal* court. Different rules may apply when plaintiffs sue state colleges and universities in the courts of their *own State,* such as when the University of Kentucky faces suit in a Kentucky state court. Suits against state colleges and universities in the courts of their own State are governed by state law. Many, if not most States have waived sovereign immunity for contract claims as well as common law tort claims up to a specific amount. Some States have waived sovereign immunity for specific statutory claims such as those prohibiting discrimination.

Yet, when state colleges or universities are sued in the courts of *another State*, sovereign immunity becomes absolute. As the Supreme Court explained, "the Constitution affirmatively altered the relationships between the States, so that they no longer relate to each other solely as foreign sovereigns. Each State's equal dignity and sovereignty under the Constitution implies certain constitutional 'limitation[s] on the sovereignty of all of its sister States.'"[136] Given "our constitutional design and the understanding of sovereign immunity shared by the States that ratified the Constitution," the only logical conclusion is States retain their sovereign immunity from private suits brought in the courts of other States.[137]

III. ACTIONS AGAINST INDIVIDUAL UNIVERSITY ADMINISTRATORS

A far reaching federal statute, commonly called "Section 1983," which imposes personal liability on any person who, while acting with the actual or apparent authority of a state or local government, violates the constitutional or statutory rights of another person.[138] More specifically, the statute says "every person who, under the color of any statute, ordinance, regulation, custom or usage" of a state or local government "subjects or causes to be subjected" another person "to the deprivation of any rights, privileges, or immunities secured by the Constitution and laws," has liability to the person injured.[139]

This statute, which originated during the Reconstruction Era to protect the newly freed slaves, provides a remedy whenever a state or local official violates a person's civil rights. Because those whose rights are violated can recover both monetary awards and attorney fees, Section 1983 offers significant protection to those whose civil rights are violated by officials at state colleges and universities.[140]

In practice, if public employees use their status as a public employee to violate the constitutional or federal statutory rights of others, then these individuals may be personally liable for damages to the others. For example, a public institution's campus police officers, who violate the constitutional rights of protesters, may be liable to the protesters. Nevertheless, in many instances, the public college or university will indemnify the employees for costs of paying the judgment and the costs of defense.

In constitutional litigation involving public colleges and universities, it is common to see Section 1983 claims against the individual administrators or faculty members. There are two types of Section 1983 suits. First there are personal capacity suits which "seek to impose personal liability upon a government official for actions he takes under color of state law."[141] Unless the governmental entity chooses to pay the judgment, the public officials will have to pay any damages awarded to others from their personal assets. Second, there are official capacity suits which "generally represent only another way of pleading an action against an entity of which the officer is an agent."[142] For all practical purposes, an official capacity suits should "be treated as suit against the entity. It is not a suit against the official personally, for the real party in interest is the entity."[143] Governmental entities will have to pay any damages awards for the public treasury.

Nevertheless, any public official, including administrators and faculty at public colleges and universities, can assert an immunity defense. Immunity defenses generally will be successful. The two types of immunity defenses—sovereign and qualified—are discussed below.

A. Sovereign Immunity for Official Capacity Claims

While a personal capacity claim against a public college or university official can result in a recovery of money damages, an official capacity claim against a public campus employee will not result in a recovery of money damages. This is so for two reasons. First, in *Will v. Michigan Department of State Police*, the Supreme Court made it clear that States are not "persons" that can be sued under Section 1983.[144] Likewise, entities that are considered an arm of the State, such as most state colleges and universities, are not "persons" under Section 1983.[145]

Second, sovereign immunity bars suit against public campus employees in their official capacities. "[A]n official capacity suit is, in all respects other than name, to be treated as a suit against the entity."[146] Therefore, sovereign immunity bars any claims against administrators in their official capacities as if the claims were against the public colleges or universities themselves.[147]

B. Qualified Immunity for Personal Capacity Claims

With respect to personal capacity claims, the public institution administrators or faculty members may have a defense of qualified immunity. The qualified immunity doctrine protects government actors "from liability for civil damages insofar as their conduct does not violate clearly established statutory or constitutional rights of which a reasonable person would have known."[148] However, the doctrine does not apply when "the constitutionality of the [state] officer's conduct is 'beyond debate.'"[149] Put another way, qualified immunity protects "all but the plainly incompetent or those who knowingly violate the law."[150]

In determining whether the official was incompetent or knowingly violated the law, courts "ask whether it would have been clear to a reasonable officer that the alleged conduct was unlawful in the situation he confronted."[151] If the answer is yes, then the officials are incompetent or knowingly violated the law and are not entitled to qualified immunity.[152] Conversely, if the answer is no, then the officials would not have known that their conduct was unlawful and would be entitled to qualified immunity.[153]

Once public officials plead qualified immunity for a Section 1983 claim, the burden is on the plaintiff to demonstrate the public official: (1) violated a constitutional or federal statutory right of the plaintiff; and, if so, (2) the violation involved a clearly established constitutional or statutory right.[154] Absent a violation of the Constitution or the law, then there is no liability and no need to address whether qualified immunity applies. Alternatively, if the plaintiffs establish that the public officials did violate the Constitution or federal statutes then the focus is "whether the officer had fair notice that her conduct was unlawful."[155] The reasonableness of the public officials' conduct "is judged against the backdrop of the law at the time of the conduct. If the law at that time did not clearly establish that the officer's conduct would violate the Constitution [or a federal statute], the officer should not be subject to liability or, indeed, even the burdens of litigation."[156] It is not enough that the rule is suggested by then-existing precedent.[157] "The precedent must be clear enough that every reasonable official would interpret it to establish the particular rule the plaintiff seeks to apply."[158]

Put another way, public college or university administrators or faculty members are not going to be held personally liable for a constitutional violation unless either the Supreme Court or the U.S. Court of Appeals for the State where the institutions are located have addressed the situation and concluded there is a violation of the Constitution or federal law.

IV. SUMMARY OF MAJOR CASES DISCUSSED IN THIS CHAPTER

Board of Trustees of University of Alabama v. Garrett, 531 U.S. 356 (2001)

The Supreme Court held Congress had not abrogated the States' sovereign immunity for claims based on Title II of the Americans with Disabilities Act. Thus, a university faculty member could not bring such a claim against a state university.

Central Virginia Community College v. Katz, 546 U.S. 356 (2006)

The Supreme Court declared the States, by ratifying the Constitution, had surrendered their sovereign immunity for In rem proceedings in bankruptcy. Therefore, sovereign immunity did not bar the adversarial proceeding a Chapter 11 trustee brought to set aside alleged preferential transfers that a debtor made to state agencies.

City of Boerne v. Flores, 521 U.S. 507 (1997)

The Supreme Court imposed significant limitations on the power of Congress to enforce the Fourteenth Amendment. *Flores* finds Congress' powers under § 5 are limited to enforcing the actual substantive guarantees of the Fourteenth Amendment, which include Equal Protection of the laws, the Privileges or Immunities of national citizenship, and Due Process. For legislation to be a valid exercise of congressional power to enforce the Fourteenth Amendment, Congress must make specific findings that the States have violated the Constitution. Even if those findings exist, the resulting legislation to enforce the Fourteenth Amendment must be a "proportionate response" to the violations. The decision makes it far more difficult for Congress to abrogate sovereign immunity.

Cooper v. Aaron, 358 U.S. 1 (1958)

The Supreme Court declared its interpretations of the Constitution were the "supreme law of the land" and its decisions bind not only the parties before the Court but similarly situated parties in later cases. Therefore, the governor and state legislature in Arkansas could not refuse to fulfill the Supreme Court's mandate to desegregate public schools.

Ex Parte Young, 209 U.S. 123 (1908)

The Supreme Court determined a federal court may hear a claim against individual state officers, such as the president of a state college or university, which seek (1) a declaratory judgment that the state officer is currently violating federal law; and (2) an injunction forcing the state official to conform his current conduct to federal law. By allowing a suit against the responsible official rather than the State itself, the Court created an exception to sovereign immunity. The *Ex Parte Young* doctrine is a method of holding state officials accountable for statutes and policies that violate federal law.

Florida Prepaid Postsecondary Education Expense Board v. College Savings Bank, 527 U.S. 627 (1999)

Because the Supreme Court determined Congress had not abrogated the States' sovereign immunity for patent claims, a private party could not sue a state agency.

Franchise Tax Board of California v. Hyatt, 139 S. Ct. 1485 (2019)

The Supreme Court declared the States have sovereign immunity in the courts of another State. The decision is significant in that it prevents most state colleges and universities from being sued in other State.

Kimel v. Florida Board of Regents, 528 U.S. 62 (2000)

The Supreme Court determined Congress had not abrogated the States' sovereign immunity for Age Discrimination in Employment Act. As a result, the faculty member could not sue this institution.

Seminole Tribe v. Florida, 517 U.S. 44 (1996)

The Supreme Court held Congress' power to abrogate sovereign immunity was limited to its efforts to enforce the Fourteenth Amendment. Phrased differently, Congress could not use its Article I powers to abolish the States' sovereign immunity. The Court also declared the *Ex Parte Young* doctrine was inapplicable in those situations where Congress had enacted a "comprehensive remedial scheme." This holding represents a limitation on the *Ex Parte Young* doctrine.

NOTES

1. THE FEDERALIST NO. 78 (Alexander Hamilton).
2. THE FEDERALIST NO. 39 (James Madison).
3. Gordon S. Wood, POWER AND LIBERTY: CONSTITUTIONALISM IN THE AMERICAN REVOLUTION 18–26, 92–95 (2021).
4. *Id.* at 48.
5. *Id.* at 47–52, 92–95.
6. U.S. Const. art VI, § 2.
7. *Marbury v. Madison,* 5 U.S. (1 Cranch) 137, 176 (1803).
8. *Cooper v. Aaron,* 358 U.S. 1, 18–19 (1958).
9. Josh Blackman, *The Irrepressible Myths of Cooper v. Aaron,* 107 GEO. L.J. 1135, 1137 (2019).
10. Stephen Breyer, MAKING OUR DEMOCRACY WORK: A JUDGE'S VIEW 60 (2010).
11. *Milliken v. Bradley,* 433 U.S. 267, 280–81 (1977).
12. Neil Gorsuch, A REPUBLIC, IF YOU CAN KEEP IT 237 (2019).
13. William A. Kaplin, Barbara A. Lee, Neal H. Hutchens, & Jacob H. Rooksby, THE LAW OF HIGHER EDUCATION 288–94 (6th ed. 2020).
14. *Kovats v. Rutgers, the State University,* 822 F.2d 1303 (3rd Cir. 1987) (holding that a public university in New Jersey was not considered the State for purposes of sovereign immunity).
15. *Ex Parte Young,* 209 U.S. 123 (1908).
16. *Id.*
17. *DeBauche v. Trani,* 191 F.3d 499, 505 (4th Cir. 1999).
18. *Green v. Mansour,* 474 U.S. 64, 68 (1985).
19. *Regan v. Time, Inc.*, 468 U.S. 641, 652 (1984) (White, J., joined by Rehnquist, C.J. & O'Connor, J., announcing the judgment of the Court).
20. *Jenkins,* 495 U.S. at 52. Cf. *Sixty–seventh Minnesota State Senate v. Beens,* 406 U.S. 187, 196, (1972) (*per curiam*).
21. *Whitcomb v. Chavis,* 403 U.S. 124, 161 (1971).
22. *Brown v. Board of Education,* 349 U.S. 294, 299 (1955).
23. *Idaho v. Coeur d'Alene Tribe,* 521 U.S. 261, 269 (1997).
24. *Id.* at 270.
25. *Seminole Tribe,* 517 U.S. at 71–75.
26. *Id.* at 71–75; *Coeur d'Alene Tribe,* 521 U.S. at 287–88.
27. 521 U.S. 261 (1997).
28. *Id.* at 287–88.
29. *Id.* at 281.
30. *Id.* at 287–88.
31. U.S. Const. amend. XI.
32. *Alden v. Maine,* 527 U.S. 706, 713, (1999).

33. *Federal Maritime Commission v. South Carolina State Ports Authority,* 535 U.S. 743, 754 (2002).
34. *United Carolina Bank v. Board of Regents of Steven F. Austin State University,* 665 F.2d 553, 558 (5th Cir. 1983).
35. Kaplin, Lee, Hutchens, Rooksby, *supra* note 12, at 288–94.
36. *Puerto Rico Aqueduct & Sewer Authority v. Metcalfe & Eddy, Inc.,* 506 U.S. 139, 145–46 (1993).
37. *Federal Maritime Commission,* 535 U.S. at 751.
38. *Id.* at 752.
39. *Alden,* 527 U.S. at 716.
40. THE FEDERALIST No. 81 (Alexander Hamilton) (emphasis original).
41. THE FEDERALIST No. 39 (James Madison).
42. *Central Virginia Community College. v. Katz,* 546 U.S. 356 (2006).
43. *Chisholm v. Georgia,* 2 U.S. (2 Dall.) 419 (1793).
44. *Id.* U.S. at 468 (Cushing, J.); 440 (Wilson, J.); 478–79 (Jay, C.J.); 450–53 (Blair, J.).
45. *Federal Maritime Commission,* 535 U.S. at 752; *Alden,* 527 U.S. at 721.
46. *Federal Maritime Commission,* 535 U.S. at 752–53; *Alden,* 527 U.S. at 721–22.
47. *Alden,* 527 U.S. at 723.
48. *Hans v. Louisiana,* 134 U.S. 1, 15 (1890).
49. *Puerto Rico Aqueduct,* 539 U.S. at 146 (1993).
50. *Blatchford v. Native Village of Noatak,* 501 U.S. 775, 779 (1991).
51. *Hess v. Port Authority Trans-Hudson Corp.,* 513 U.S. 30, 48 (1994).
52. *Puerto Rico Aqueduct,* 506 U.S. at 146 (internal quotation marks omitted).
53. *Alden,* 527 U.S. at 733.
54. *Blatchford,* 501 U.S. at 782.
55. *Principality of Monaco v. Mississippi,* 292 U.S. 313, 330–32 (1934).
56. *Smith v. Reeves,* 178 U.S. 436, 446, 449 (1900).
57. *Alden,* 527 U.S. at 712.
58. *Federal Maritime Commission,* 535 U.S. at 760.
59. *In re New York,* 256 U.S. 490, 503 (1921).
60. *Doe v. Regents of the University of California,* 519 U.S. 425, 431 (1997).
61. *Federal Maritime Commission,* 535 U.S. at 755.
62. *Fitzpatrick v. Bitzer,* 427 U.S. 445 (1976).
63. *Pennsylvania v. Union Gas,* 491 U.S. 1, 14–23 (1989).
64. *Id.* at 38–56 (Scalia, J., dissenting).
65. *See, e.g.,* 42 U.S.C. § 2000d-7(a)(1) (attempting to abrogate sovereign immunity or exact a waiver of sovereign immunity for numerous statutes).
66. *Seminole Tribe,* 517 U.S. at 56–71.
67. *See Katzenbach v. Morgan,* 384 U.S. 641, 651 (1966); *Ex parte Virginia,* 100 U.S. 339, 345–346 (1880).
68. *City of Borene v. Flores,* 521 U.S. 507 (1997).
69. *Kimel v. Florida Board of Regents,* 528 U.S. 62 (2000).
70. *Board of Trustees of University of Alabama v. Garrett,* 531 U.S. 356 (2001).
71. *Federal Maritime Commission,* 535 U.S. at 753.

72. *Coleman v. Court of Appeals of Maryland*, 566 U.S. 30 (2012).
73. *Allen v. Cooper*, 140 S. Ct. 994 (2020).
74. *Nevada Dep't of Human Resources v. Hibbs*, 538 U.S. 721 (2003).
75. *Tennessee Student Asst. Corp. v. Hood*, 541 U.S. 440 (2004).
76. *Tennessee v. Lane*, 541 U.S. 509 (2004).
77. *United States v. Georgia*, 546 U.S. 151 (2006).
78. *Id.* at 158.
79. *Kimel*, 528 U.S. at 78–80.
80. *Id.* at 80.
81. *Id.*
82. *Marbury v. Madison*, 5 U.S. (1 Cranch) 137, 176 (1803).
83. *New York*, 505 U.S. at 156–57.
84. *Seminole Tribe*, 517 U.S. at 73.
85. *Kimel*, 528 U.S. at 78.
86. *Seminole Tribe*, 517 U.S. at 72.
87. Similarly, the Thirteenth, Fifteenth, Nineteenth, Twenty-third, Twenty-fourth, and Twenty-sixth Amendments contain provisions that allow Congress to enforce these Amendments against the States. *See* U.S. Const. amends. XIII, § 2; XV, § 2; XIX § 2; XXIII, § 2; XXIV, § 2; XXVI, § 2.
88. *See Johnson v. California*, 125 S. Ct. 1141, 1146 (2005) (Equal Protection); *Saenz*, 526 U.S. at 503–4 (Privileges or Immunities).
89. *Barron v. Mayor of Baltimore*, 32 U.S. (7 Pet.) 243, 249 (1833).
90. *McDonald v. City of Chicago, Ill.*, 561 U.S. 742, 764–65 nn. 12–13(2010).
91. *Flores*, 521 U.S. at 519–20.
92. *Kimel*, 528 U.S. at 81.
93. *Fitzpatrick*, 427 U.S. at 456 (citation omitted).
94. *Dellmuth v. Muth*, 491 U.S. 223, 227–28 (1989).
95. *Lane*, 541 U.S. at 518; *Nevada Department of Human Resources v. Hibbs*, 538 U.S. 721, 726 (2003); *Garrett*, 531 U.S. at 364; *Kimel*, 528 U.S. at 80; *Alden*, 527 U.S. at 756; *College Savings Bank v. Florida Prepaid Postsecondary Educational Expense Board*, 527 U.S. 666, 670 (1999); *Florida Prepaid Postsecondary Educational Expense Board v. College Savings Bank*, 527 U.S. 627, 637 (1999); *Seminole Tribe*, 517 U.S. at 59.
96. *Seminole Tribe*, 517 U.S. at 58–65.
97. *Id.* at 56–59.
98. *Humenansky v. Regents of the University of Minnesota*, 152 F.3d 822, 824 (8th Cir. 1998).
99. *Kimel*, 528 U.S. at 78.
100. *Garrett*, 531 U.S. at 365–74.
101. *Id.* at 365.
102. *Hibbs*, 538 U.S. at 736.
103. *See* Erwin Chemerinsky, *Unanswered Questions: October Term 2003*, 7 GREENBAG 2ND 323, 329 (2004).
104. *Garrett*, 531 U.S. at 368.
105. *College Savings Bank*, 527 U.S. at 675.

106. *Florida Prepaid,* 527 U.S. at 646.
107. *Madison v. Virginia,* 474 F.3d 118, 129 (4th Cir. 2006).
108. *College Savings Bank,* 527 U.S. at 670.
109. *Edelman v. Jordan,* 415 U.S. 651, 673 (1974) (citation omitted).
110. *Smith v. Reeves,* 178 U.S. 436, 441–45 (1900).
111. *Florida Dep't of Health and Rehabilitative Services v. Florida Nursing Home Association,* 450 U.S. 147, 149–50 (1981) (*per curiam*).
112. *Kennecott Copper Corp. v. State Tax Commission,* 327 U.S. 573, 577–79 (1946).
113. *Atascadero,* 473 U.S. at 241 (citations omitted).
114. *College Savings Bank,* 527 U.S. at 681–84.
115. *Atascadero,* 473 U.S. at 246–47.
116. *United States v. Butler,* 297 U.S. 1, 75 (1936).
117. *South Dakota v. Dole,* 483 U.S. 203, 207 (1987).
118. U.S. Const. art I., § 8, cl. 1.
119. *Dole,* 483 U.S. at 217 (O'Connor, J., joined by Brennan, J., dissenting).
120. Lynn A. Baker, *The Revival of States' Rights: A Progress Report and a Proposal,* 22 Harv. J.L. & Pub. Pol. 95, 100–101 (1998).
121. 42 U.S.C. § 2000d-7.
122. *See, e.g., Constantine v. Rector & Visitors of George Mason University,* 411 F.3d 474, 492–94 (4th Cir. 2005) *Cherry v. University of Wisconsin,* 265 F.3d 541, 554 (7th Cir. 2001); *Pederson v. Louisiana State University,* 213 F.3d 858, 875–876 (5th Cir. 2000); *Litman v. George Mason University,* 186 F.3d 544, 554 (4th Cir. 1999).
123. *Nat'l Fed'n of Indep. Bus. v. Sebelius,* 567 U.S. 519, 580 (2012).
124. *Id.*
125. *Id.*
126. *See Oklahoma Tax Commission v. Citizen Band Potawatomi Tribe,* 498 U.S. 505, 509 (1991); *United States v. United States Fidelity & Guaranty Co.,* 309 U.S. at 511–12; *United States v. Shaw,* 309 U.S. 495, 501–2 (1940).
127. *Gardner v. New Jersey,* 329 U.S. 565, 573–74 (1947).
128. Karen Cordry, *Seminole Seven Years on,* in Annual Survey of Bankruptcy Law 2002–2003 383, 455 (William L. Norton ed., 2003). *See also* Dan Schweitzer, *LaPides v. Board of Regents of the University of Georgia System: A Partial Answer to the Sovereign Immunity-Waiver Conundrum,* 17 Nat'l Envir. L.J. 3 (Dec. 2002/Jan 2003).
129. *Potawatomi Tribe,* 498 U.S. at 509; *United States Fidelity & Guaranty Co.,* 309 U.S. at 513.
130. *Potawatomi Tribe,* 498 U.S. at 509.
131. *Gardner,* 329 U.S. at 574.
132. *Shaw,* 309 U.S. at 501.
133. *Lapides v. Board of Regents of the University System of Georgia,* 535 U.S. 613, 617 (2002).
134. *See Stroud v. McIntosh,* 722 F.3d 1294, 1302 (11th Cir. 2013); *Bergemann v. Rhode Island Department of Environmental Management.,* 665 F.3d 336, 342 (1st Cir. 2011); *Lombardo v. Pennsylvania. Department of Public Welfare,* 540 F.3d 190, 198

(3rd Cir. 2008); *Meyers ex rel. Benzing v. Texas,* 410 F.3d 236, 255 (5th Cir. 2005); *Stewart v. North Carolina,* 393 F.3d 484, 490 (4th Cir. 2005); *Watters v. Washington Metropolitan Transit Authority.,* 295 F.3d 36, 39, 42 n. 13 (D.C. Cir. 2002).

135. *Beaulieu v. Vermont,* 807 F.3d 478, 488 (2nd Cir. 2015).
136. *Franchise Tax Board of California v. Hyatt,* 139 S. Ct. 1485, 1497 (2019).
137. *Id.* at 1492.
138. 42 U.S.C. § 1983.
139. *Id.*
140. 42 U.S.C. § 1988 (recovery of attorney fees).
141. *Kentucky v. Graham,* 473 U.S. 159, 165 (1985).
142. *Monell v. New York City Department of Social Services,* 436 U.S. 658, 690 n. 55 (1978).
143. *Graham,* 473 U.S. at 166.
144. *Will v. Michigan Department of State Police,* 491 U.S. 58, 64 (1989).
145. *Hutsell v. Sayre,* 5 F.3d 996, 999 (6th Cir. 1993).
146. *Kentucky v. Graham,* 473 U.S. 159, 166 (1985).
147. *Hutsell,* 5 F.3d at 1002–1003.
148. *Harlow v. Fitzgerald,* 457 U.S. 800, 818 (1982).
149. *District of Columbia v. Wesby,* 138 S.Ct. 577, 589 (2018).
150. *Malley v. Briggs,* 475 U.S. 335, 341 (1986).
151. *Ziglar v. Abbasi,* 137 S. Ct. 1843, 1867 (2017).
152. *Id.*
153. *Id.*
154. *Pearson v. Callahan,* 555 U.S. 223, 236 (2009).
155. *Brosseau v. Haugen,* 543 U.S. 194, 198 (2004).
156. *Id.*
157. *Wesby,* 138 S. Ct. at 590.
158. *Id.*

Conclusion

But There Is Us: Public Higher Education and Hope for the Constitution

> There is no vaccination against ignorance, but there is us. There is this University. And we still have heavy doors to open, unmet obligations to the land and its people. There are still leadership opportunities to advance . . . this nation, and our world towards fulling its potential, towards meeting its lofty promises.—Frank X. Walker[1]

America is defined not by race, blood, soil, religion, language, or culture, but by "the belief in the principles of equality and freedom this country stands for."[2] As President Biden observed, "America is unique. Unlike every other nation on Earth, we were founded based on an idea. We hold these truths to be self-evident: that all people are created equal, endowed by their creator with certain unalienable rights—among them life, liberty, and the pursuit of happiness."[3]

In Lincoln's words, a Nation "conceived in liberty and dedicated to the proposition that all . . . are created equal."[4] This is the "promissory note to which every American was to fall heir."[5] While We the People often have failed to live up to these self-evident truths, "we have never given up on them."[6] Indeed, "every generation of Americans has expanded wider and wider to include those who were excluded before."[7] Nevertheless, the self-evident truths are insecure and "never more than one generation away from extinction."[8]

To secure the self-evident truths, the People, in the exercise of their sovereignty, established a Constitution that controls both the governed and those who govern.[9] As the words of the Constitution represent the overwhelming consensus of the sovereign People, the Constitution is effectively sovereign.[10] If "the will of the [government], declared in its statutes [and executive actions], stands in opposition to that of the people, declared in the Constitution," the Constitution prevails.[11]

To control those who govern, our Constitution "withdraws certain subjects from the vicissitudes of political controversy,"[12] prevents the concentration of "power in one location as an expedient solution to the crisis of the day,"[13] and established "two orders of government [federal and state], each with its own direct relationship, its own privity, its own set of mutual rights and obligations to the people who sustain it and are governed by it."[14] Therefore, if the Constitution is "interpreted, as it ought to be interpreted, the Constitution is a glorious liberty document."[15]

Yet, in the third decade of the third millennium, many Americans doubt the self-evident truths foreshadowed by the *Mayflower* passengers,[16] declared by the colonies at Philadelphia,[17] confirmed by Lincoln at Gettysburg,[18] and reiterated by King on the steps of the Lincoln Memorial.[19] The constitutional consensus that once defined our Republic nears collapse. Many on both the Left and Right now doubt the value of Free Speech, Religious Liberty, Due Process, and Equal Protection. Our Nation lacks "agreement about the purpose of our country, the nature of the common good, and the meaning of human flourishing."[20]

Instead of a Union conceived in Liberty and dedicated to the Proposition that all are created Equal, we seem to be dividing into Tribes that Fear Freedom and Endorse Intersectionality. We live in bubbles—our communities are solidly red or blue, our neighborhoods consist of people with similar incomes, and our circle of friends is predominately People of Faith or Citizens of the Secular.

Instead of civil discourse, we engage in high-tech name calling, fight twitter wars, troll each other, speak in absolutes, cancel what is questionable or disagreeable, reduce complexity to simple terms, and ignore subtle, yet crucial distinctions. It seems many Americans have forgotten a basic truth: "Freedom flows from the tireless efforts of those who proclaim and pursue protection of the equal human dignity of all."[21] It seems "there is not a single important cultural, religious, political or social force that is pulling Americans together more than it is pushing us apart."[22] The future of the Constitution and the Nation it defines looks precarious.

"But there is us."[23] There are America's public colleges and universities. Our campuses are a microcosm of the Nation. The typical state flagship university has students from every county within its State, from every other State, and from all six continents. Every race, ethnicity, sex, age group, sexual orientation, gender identity, and disability status is represented. Some are from the inner city, and some are from towns without stoplights. A substantial number of students come from poverty, but they attend alongside the children of multimillionaires. Many have lived in multiple States or even overseas; a few have never left their home State. Some students may be the first in their families to attend higher education while others come from four generations of alumni. If one walks across a state university campus, one will see gay pride t-shirts and students wearing traditional religious garb. Student organizations stand for seemingly every political perspective and religious faith. The rhetoric of our students is often rough rather than refined; provocative rather than precise; inflammatory rather insightful.

In such a diverse environment, there is much potential for conflict over values and beliefs that many view as fundamental, but there is a possibility of learning "to be steadfast in our personal convictions, while also making room for the cacophony that may ensue when others disagree with us."[24] Like the K–12 public schools, America's public campuses "are the nurseries of democracy. Our representative democracy only works if we protect the 'marketplace of ideas.' This free exchange facilitates an informed public opinion, which, when transmitted to lawmakers, helps produce laws that reflect the People's will."[25] Public institutions "have a strong interest in ensuring that future generations understand the workings in practice" of Free Speech, Religious Liberty, Equal Protection, and Due Process.[26]

When officials at our public institutions adhere to the Constitution, campuses become places "of facilitating disagreement across differences."[27] Despite our differing backgrounds, cultures, views, and experiences, every American is "seeking a home where he himself is free."[28] Campuses must tolerate the "freedom to say almost anything to anyone,"[29] while also insisting all "have dignity in their own distinct identity."[30] Administrators must affirm that everyone, regardless of status, "is a member of the community too"[31] and cannot be "treated as social outcasts or as inferior in dignity and worth."[32] Institutional leaders must promote the "nobility and dignity [of] all persons, without regard to their station in life,"[33] while recognizing their communities have room "both for you and 'a man whose words make your blood boil, who's standing center stage and advocating at the top of his lungs that which you would spend a lifetime opposing at the top of yours.'"[34]

When officials at public campuses embrace the Constitution, they advance human knowledge. Because "many commonly accepted views have proved mistaken, while many ostracized views have illuminated the path toward truth," everyone must "remain free to inquire, to study and to evaluate, to gain new maturity and understanding; otherwise our civilization will stagnate and die."[35] The questions of the day will be resolved by facts, not feelings; by science, not superstition; by debate, not dogma; by discussion, not denunciation; by heterodoxy, not orthodoxy.

State colleges and universities where the leaders follow the Constitution are our best hope "to transform the jangling discords of our Nation into a beautiful symphony."[36] Our young adults can learn the importance of Free Speech, Religious Liberty, Equal Protection, and Due Process, at both the federal and state levels, at a time when they are just beginning their participation in America's civic life.

Our campus communities can realize the United States is "wide enough" for red states and blue states, urban and rural, the secular and the sacred, the new immigrant and the Tribal Nations, the descendants of slaves and the descendants of pilgrims, People of Faith and people of no faith, those who remember Pearl Harbor and those who do not remember 9-11, the critical race theorist and the constitutional originalist, the gay and the straight, the cisgender and the transgender/nonbinary.[37] If students, faculty, and staff learn and implement the Constitution's lessons of Freedom and Equality on our public college and university campuses, then an imperfect People's journey toward a "more perfect union" will continue.

NOTES

1. Frank X. Walker, SEEDTIME IN THE COMMONWEALTH: ON THE OCCASION OF THE UNIVERSITY OF KENTUCKY'S SESQUICENTENNIAL (2015).

2. Antonin Scalia, *What Makes an American* in Scalia Speaks: REFLECTIONS ON LAW, FAITH, AND LIFE WELL LIVED 15, 17 (Christopher J. Scalia & Edward Whelan, eds. 2017).

3. Joseph Biden, Remarks by President Biden Celebrating Independence Day and Independence from Covid 19 (2021).

4. Abraham Lincoln, GETTYSBURG ADDRESS (1863).

5. Martin Luther King, I Have A Dream (1963).

6. Joseph Biden, Remarks by President Biden Celebrating Independence Day and Independence from Covid 19 (2021).

7. *Id.*

8. Ronald Reagan, A TIME FOR CHOOSING (1964).

9. THE FEDERALIST No. 51 (James Madison).

10. Gordon S. Wood, POWER AND LIBERTY: CONSTITUTIONALISM IN THE AMERICAN REVOLUTION 47–52, 92–95 (2021).

11. THE FEDERALIST No. 78 (Alexander Hamilton).

12. *Barnette*, 319 U.S. at 638.

13. *New York v. United States*, 505 U.S. 144, 187 (1992).

14. *U.S. Term Limits v. Thornton*, 514 U.S. 779, 838 (1995) (Kennedy, J. concurring).

15. Frederick Douglass, WHAT TO THE SLAVE IS THE FOURTH OF JULY (1852).

16. Mayflower COMPACT (1620).

17. Declaration of Independence.
18. Abraham Lincoln, Gettysburg Address (1863).
19. Martin Luther King, I Have A Dream (1963).
20. John Inazu & Tim Keller, *Introduction* in UNCOMMON GROUND: LIVING FAITHFULLY IN A WORLD OF DIFFERENCE xv, xv (John Inazu & Tim Keller, eds. 2020).
21. Danielle Allen, *The Constitution Counted My Great-Great Grandfather as Three-Fifths of a Free Person, Here's Why I Love It Anyway*, ATLANTIC 58, 62 (October 2020).
22. David French, DIVIDED WE FALL: AMERICA'S SECESSION THREAT AND HOW TO RESTORE OUR NATION 1–2 (2020).
23. Frank X. Walker, SEEDTIME IN THE COMMONWEALTH: ON THE OCCASION OF THE UNIVERSITY OF KENTUCKY'S SESQUICENTENNIAL (2015).
24. John D. Inazu, CONFIDENT PLURALISM: SURVIVING AND THRIVING THROUGH DEEP DIFFERENCE 8 (2016).
25. *Mahanoy Area School District v. B. L.*, 141 S. Ct. 2038, 2046 (2021).
26. *Id.*
27. John Inazu, *The Purpose (and Limits) of the University*, 2018 UTAH L. REV. 943, 947 (2018).
28. Langston Hughes, LET AMERICA BE AMERICA AGAIN (1935).
29. John D. Inazu, CONFIDENT PLURALISM: SURVIVING AND THRIVING THROUGH DEEP DIFFERENCE 96 (2016).
30. *Obergefell v. Hodges*, 576 U.S. 644, 660 (2015).
31. *Trinity Lutheran Church of Columbia, Inc. v. Comer*, 137 S. Ct. 2012, 2022 (2017).
32. *Masterpiece Cakeshop, Ltd. v. Colorado Civil Rights Commission*, 138 S. Ct. 1719, 1727 (2018).
33. *Obergefell*, 576 U.S. at 656.
34. *Chelsey Nelson Photography LLC v. Louisville/Jefferson County. Metro Gov't*, 479 F. Supp. 3d 543, 548 (W.D. Ky. 2020).
35. University of Virginia, Statement of the Committee on Free Expression & Free Inquiry (2021).
36. Martin Luther King, I Have a Dream (1963).
37. Lin-Manuel Miranda, *The World Was Wide Enough* (2015) (penultimate song in the musical Hamilton (2015)).

Appendix A

The Constitution of the United States

WE THE PEOPLE of the United States, in Order to form a more perfect Union, establish Justice, ensure domestic Tranquility, provide for the common defense, promote the general Welfare, and secure the Blessings of Liberty to ourselves and our Posterity, do ordain and establish this Constitution for the United States of America.

ARTICLE I

Section 1

All legislative Powers herein granted shall be vested in a Congress of the United States, which shall consist of a Senate and House of Representatives.

Section 2

1. The House of Representatives shall be composed of Members chosen every second Year by the People of the several States, and the Electors in each State shall have the Qualifications requisite for Electors of the most numerous Branch of the State Legislature.
2. No Person shall be a Representative who shall not have attained to the Age of twenty-five Years, and been seven Years a Citizen of the United States, and who shall not, when elected, be an Inhabitant of that State in which he shall be chosen.
3. Representatives and direct Taxes shall be apportioned among the several States which may be included within this Union, according to their respective Numbers, which shall be determined by adding to the whole Number of free Persons, including those bound to Service for a

Term of Years, and excluding Indians not taxed, three fifths of all other Persons. The actual Enumeration shall be made within three Years after the first Meeting of the Congress of the United States, and within every subsequent Term of ten Years, in such Manner as they shall by Law direct. The Number of Representatives shall not exceed one for every thirty Thousand, but each State shall have at Least one Representative; and until such enumeration shall be made, the State of New Hampshire shall be entitled to choose three, Massachusetts eight, Rhode-Island and Providence Plantations one, Connecticut five, New-York six, New Jersey four, Pennsylvania eight, Delaware one, Maryland six, Virginia ten, North Carolina five, South Carolina five, and Georgia three.

4. When vacancies happen in the Representation from any State, the Executive Authority thereof shall issue Writs of Election to fill such Vacancies.
5. The House of Representatives shall choose their Speaker and other Officers; and shall have the sole Power of Impeachment.

Section 3

1. The Senate of the United States shall be composed of two Senators from each State, chosen by the Legislature thereof, for six Years; and each Senator shall have one Vote.
2. Immediately after they shall be assembled in Consequence of the first Election, they shall be divided as equally as may be into three Classes. The Seats of the Senators of the first Class shall be vacated at the Expiration of the second Year, of the second Class at the Expiration of the fourth Year, and of the third Class at the Expiration of the sixth Year, so that one third may be chosen every second Year; and if Vacancies happen by Resignation, or otherwise, during the Recess of the Legislature of any State, the Executive thereof may make temporary Appointments until the next Meeting of the Legislature, which shall then fill such Vacancies.
3. No Person shall be a Senator who shall not have attained to the Age of thirty Years, and been nine Years a Citizen of the United States, and who shall not, when elected, be an Inhabitant of that State for which he shall be chosen.
4. The Vice President of the United States shall be President of the Senate, but shall have no Vote, unless they be equally divided.
5. The Senate shall choose their other Officers, and also a President pro tempore, in the Absence of the Vice President, or when he shall exercise the Office of President of the United States.

6. The Senate shall have the sole Power to try all Impeachments. When sitting for that Purpose, they shall be on Oath or Affirmation. When the President of the United States is tried, the Chief Justice shall preside: And no Person shall be convicted without the Concurrence of two thirds of the Members present.
7. Judgment in Cases of Impeachment shall not extend further than to removal from Office, and disqualification to hold and enjoy any Office of honor, Trust or Profit under the United States: but the Party convicted shall nevertheless be liable and subject to Indictment, Trial, Judgment and Punishment, according to Law.

Section 4

1. The Times, Places and Manner of holding Elections for Senators and Representatives, shall be prescribed in each State by the Legislature thereof; but the Congress may at any time by Law make or alter such Regulations, except as to the Places of choosing Senators.
2. The Congress shall assemble at least once in every Year, and such Meeting shall be on the first Monday in December, unless they shall by Law appoint a different Day.

Section 5

1. Each House shall be the Judge of the Elections, Returns and Qualifications of its own Members, and a Majority of each shall constitute a Quorum to do Business; but a smaller Number may adjourn from day to day, and may be authorized to compel the Attendance of absent Members, in such Manner, and under such Penalties as each House may provide.
2. Each House may determine the Rules of its Proceedings, punish its Members for disorderly Behavior, and, with the Concurrence of two thirds, expel a Member.
3. Each House shall keep a Journal of its Proceedings, and from time to time publish the same, excepting such Parts as may in their Judgment require Secrecy; and the Yeas and Nays of the Members of either House on any question shall, at the Desire of one fifth of those Present, be entered on the Journal.
4. Neither House, during the Session of Congress, shall, without the Consent of the other, adjourn for more than three days, nor to any other Place than that in which the two Houses shall be sitting.

Section 6

1. The Senators and Representatives shall receive a Compensation for their Services, to be ascertained by Law, and paid out of the Treasury of the United States. They shall in all Cases, except Treason, Felony and Breach of the Peace, be privileged from Arrest during their Attendance at the Session of their respective Houses, and in going to and returning from the same; and for any Speech or Debate in either House, they shall not be questioned in any other Place.
2. No Senator or Representative shall, during the Time for which he was elected, be appointed to any civil Office under the Authority of the United States, which shall have been created, or the Emoluments whereof shall have been increased during such time; and no Person holding any Office under the United States, shall be a Member of either House during his Continuance in Office.

Section 7

1. All Bills for raising Revenue shall originate in the House of Representatives; but the Senate may propose or concur with Amendments as on other Bills.
2. Every Bill which shall have passed the House of Representatives and the Senate, shall, before it become a Law, be presented to the President of the United States; If he approve he shall sign it, but if not he shall return it, with his Objections to that House in which it shall have originated, who shall enter the Objections at large on their Journal, and proceed to reconsider it. If after such Reconsideration two thirds of that House shall agree to pass the Bill, it shall be sent, together with the Objections, to the other House, by which it shall likewise be reconsidered, and if approved by two thirds of that House, it shall become a Law. But in all such Cases the Votes of both Houses shall be determined by yeas and Nays, and the Names of the Persons voting for and against the Bill shall be entered on the Journal of each House, respectively. If any Bill shall not be returned by the President within ten Days (Sundays excepted) after it shall have been presented to him, the Same shall be a Law, in like Manner as if he had signed it, unless the Congress by their Adjournment prevent its Return, in which Case it shall not be a Law.
3. Every Order, Resolution, or Vote to which the Concurrence of the Senate and House of Representatives may be necessary (except on a question of Adjournment) shall be presented to the President of the United States; and before the Same shall take Effect, shall be approved by him, or being disapproved by him, shall be repassed by two thirds

of the Senate and House of Representatives, according to the Rules and Limitations prescribed in the Case of a Bill.

Section 8

1. The Congress shall have Power To lay and collect Taxes, Duties, Imposts and Excises, to pay the Debts and provide for the common Defense and general Welfare of the United States; but all Duties, Imposts and Excises shall be uniform throughout the United States;
2. To borrow Money on the credit of the United States;
3. To regulate Commerce with foreign Nations, and among the several States, and with the Indian Tribes;
4. To establish an uniform Rule of Naturalization, and uniform Laws on the subject of Bankruptcies throughout the United States;
5. To coin Money, regulate the Value thereof, and of foreign Coin, and fix the Standard of Weights and Measures;
6. To provide for the Punishment of counterfeiting the Securities and current Coin of the United States;
7. To establish Post Offices and post Roads;
8. To promote the Progress of Science and useful Arts, by securing for limited Times to Authors and Inventors the exclusive Right to their respective Writings and Discoveries;
9. To constitute Tribunals inferior to the supreme Court;
10. To define and punish Piracies and Felonies committed on the high Seas, and Offences against the Law of Nations;
11. To declare War, grant Letters of Marque and Reprisal, and make Rules concerning Captures on Land and Water;
12. To raise and support Armies, but no Appropriation of Money to that Use shall be for a longer Term than two Years;
13. To provide and maintain a Navy;
14. To make Rules for the Government and Regulation of the land and naval Forces;
15. To provide for calling forth the Militia to execute the Laws of the Union, suppress Insurrections and repel Invasions;
16. To provide for organizing, arming, and disciplining, the Militia, and for governing such Part of them as may be employed in the Service of the United States, reserving to the States respectively, the Appointment of the Officers, and the Authority of training the Militia according to the discipline prescribed by Congress;
17. To exercise exclusive Legislation in all Cases whatsoever, over such District (not exceeding ten Miles square) as may, by Cession of particular States, and the Acceptance of Congress, become the Seat of the

Government of the United States, and to exercise like Authority over all Places purchased by the Consent of the Legislature of the State in which the Same shall be, for the Erection of Forts, Magazines, Arsenals, dock-Yards, and other needful Buildings;—And

18. To make all Laws which shall be necessary and proper for carrying into Execution the foregoing Powers, and all other Powers vested by this Constitution in the Government of the United States, or in any Department or Officer thereof.

Section 9

1. The Migration or Importation of such Persons as any of the States now existing shall think proper to admit, shall not be prohibited by the Congress prior to the Year one thousand eight hundred and eight, but a Tax or duty may be imposed on such Importation, not exceeding ten dollars for each Person.
2. The Privilege of the Writ of Habeas Corpus shall not be suspended, unless when in Cases of Rebellion or Invasion the public Safety may require it.
3. No Bill of Attainder or ex post facto Law shall be passed.
4. No Capitation, or other direct, Tax shall be laid, unless in Proportion to the Census or Enumeration herein before directed to be taken.
5. No Tax or Duty shall be laid on Articles exported from any State.
6. No Preference shall be given by any Regulation of Commerce or Revenue to the Ports of one State over those of another: nor shall Vessels bound to, or from, one State, be obliged to enter, clear, or pay Duties in another.
7. No Money shall be drawn from the Treasury, but in Consequence of Appropriations made by Law; and a regular Statement and Account of the Receipts and Expenditures of all public Money shall be published from time to time.
8. No Title of Nobility shall be granted by the United States: And no Person holding any Office of Profit or Trust under them, shall, without the Consent of the Congress, accept of any present, Emolument, Office, or Title, of any kind whatever, from any King, Prince, or foreign State.

Section 10

1. No State shall enter into any Treaty, Alliance, or Confederation; grant Letters of Marque and Reprisal; coin Money; emit Bills of Credit; make any Thing but gold and silver Coin a Tender in Payment of Debts;

pass any Bill of Attainder, ex post facto Law, or Law impairing the Obligation of Contracts, or grant any Title of Nobility.
2. No State shall, without the Consent of the Congress, lay any Imposts or Duties on Imports or Exports, except what may be absolutely necessary for executing its inspection Laws: and the net Produce of all Duties and Imposts, laid by any State on Imports or Exports, shall be for the Use of the Treasury of the United States; and all such Laws shall be subject to the Revision and Control of the Congress.
3. No State shall, without the Consent of Congress, lay any Duty of Tonnage, keep Troops, or Ships of War in time of Peace, enter into any Agreement or Compact with another State, or with a foreign Power, or engage in War, unless actually invaded, or in such imminent Danger as will not admit of delay.

ARTICLE II

Section 1

1. The executive Power shall be vested in a President of the United States of America. He shall hold his Office during the Term of four Years, and, together with the Vice President, chosen for the same Term, be elected, as follows.
2. Each State shall appoint, in such Manner as the Legislature thereof may direct, a Number of Electors, equal to the whole Number of Senators and Representatives to which the State may be entitled in the Congress: but no Senator or Representative, or Person holding an Office of Trust or Profit under the United States, shall be appointed an Elector.
3. The Electors shall meet in their respective States, and vote by Ballot for two Persons, of whom one at least shall not be an Inhabitant of the same State with themselves. And they shall make a List of all the Persons voted for, and of the Number of Votes for each; which List they shall sign and certify, and transmit sealed to the Seat of the Government of the United States, directed to the President of the Senate. The President of the Senate shall, in the Presence of the Senate and House of Representatives, open all the Certificates, and the Votes shall then be counted. The Person having the greatest Number of Votes shall be the President, if such Number be a Majority of the whole Number of Electors appointed; and if there be more than one who have such Majority, and have an equal Number of Votes, then the House of Representatives shall immediately choose by Ballot one of them for President; and if no Person have a Majority, then from the five highest

on the List the said House shall in like Manner choose the President. But in choosing the President, the Votes shall be taken by States, the Representation from each State having one Vote; A quorum for this Purpose shall consist of a Member or Members from two thirds of the States, and a Majority of all the States shall be necessary to a Choice. In every Case, after the Choice of the President, the Person having the greatest Number of Votes of the Electors shall be the Vice President. But if there should remain two or more who have equal Votes, the Senate shall choose from them by Ballot the Vice President.
4. The Congress may determine the Time of choosing the Electors, and the Day on which they shall give their Votes; which Day shall be the same throughout the United States.
5. No Person except a natural born Citizen, or a Citizen of the United States, at the time of the Adoption of this Constitution, shall be eligible to the Office of President; neither shall any Person be eligible to that Office who shall not have attained to the Age of thirty-five Years, and been fourteen Years a Resident within the United States.
6. In Case of the Removal of the President from Office, or of his Death, Resignation, or Inability to discharge the Powers and Duties of the said Office, the Same shall devolve on the Vice President, and the Congress may by Law provide for the Case of Removal, Death, Resignation or Inability, both of the President and Vice President, declaring what Officer shall then act as President, and such Officer shall act accordingly, until the Disability be removed, or a President shall be elected.
7. The President shall, at stated Times, receive for his Services, a Compensation, which shall neither be increased nor diminished during the Period for which he shall have been elected, and he shall not receive within that Period any other Emolument from the United States, or any of them.
8. Before he enters on the Execution of his Office, he shall take the following Oath or Affirmation:—"I do solemnly swear (or affirm) that I will faithfully execute the Office of President of the United States, and will to the best of my Ability, preserve, protect and defend the Constitution of the United States."

Section 2

1. The President shall be Commander in Chief of the Army and Navy of the United States, and of the Militia of the several States, when called into the actual Service of the United States; he may require the Opinion, in writing, of the principal Officer in each of the executive Departments, upon any Subject relating to the Duties of their respective Offices,

and he shall have Power to grant Reprieves and Pardons for Offences against the United States, except in Cases of Impeachment.
2. He shall have Power, by and with the Advice and Consent of the Senate, to make Treaties, provided two thirds of the Senators present concur; and he shall nominate, and by and with the Advice and Consent of the Senate, shall appoint Ambassadors, other public Ministers and Consuls, Judges of the supreme Court, and all other Officers of the United States, whose Appointments are not herein otherwise provided for, and which shall be established by Law: but the Congress may by Law vest the Appointment of such inferior Officers, as they think proper, in the President alone, in the Courts of Law, or in the Heads of Departments.
3. The President shall have Power to fill up all Vacancies that may happen during the Recess of the Senate, by granting Commissions which shall expire at the End of their next Session.

Section 3

He shall from time to time give to the Congress Information of the State of the Union, and recommend to their Consideration such Measures as he shall judge necessary and expedient; he may, on extraordinary Occasions, convene both Houses, or either of them, and in Case of Disagreement between them, with Respect to the Time of Adjournment, he may adjourn them to such Time as he shall think proper; he shall receive Ambassadors and other public Ministers; he shall take Care that the Laws be faithfully executed, and shall Commission all the Officers of the United States.

Section 4

The President, Vice President, and all civil Officers of the United States, shall be removed from Office on Impeachment for, and Conviction of, Treason, Bribery, or other high Crimes and Misdemeanors.

ARTICLE III

Section 1

The judicial Power of the United States shall be vested in one supreme Court, and in such inferior Courts as the Congress may from time to time ordain and establish. The Judges, both of the supreme and inferior Courts, shall hold their Offices during good Behavior, and shall, at stated Times, receive for their Services, a Compensation, which shall not be diminished during their Continuance in Office.

Section 2

1. The judicial Power shall extend to all Cases, in Law and Equity, arising under this Constitution, the Laws of the United States, and Treaties made, or which shall be made, under their Authority;—to all Cases affecting Ambassadors, other public Ministers and Consuls;—to all Cases of admiralty and maritime Jurisdiction;—to Controversies to which the United States shall be a Party;—to Controversies between two or more States;—between a State and Citizens of another State;—between Citizens of different States,—between Citizens of the same State claiming Lands under Grants of different States, and between a State, or the Citizens thereof, and foreign States, Citizens or Subjects.
2. In all Cases affecting Ambassadors, other public Ministers and Consuls, and those in which a State shall be Party, the supreme Court shall have original Jurisdiction. In all the other Cases before mentioned, the supreme Court shall have appellate Jurisdiction, both as to Law and Fact, with such Exceptions, and under such Regulations as the Congress shall make.
3. The Trial of all Crimes, except in Cases of Impeachment, shall be by Jury; and such Trial shall be held in the State where the said Crimes shall have been committed; but when not committed within any State, the Trial shall be at such Place or Places as the Congress may by Law have directed.

Section 3

1. Treason against the United States shall consist only in levying War against them, or in adhering to their Enemies, giving them Aid and Comfort. No Person shall be convicted of Treason unless on the Testimony of two Witnesses to the same overt Act, or on Confession in open Court.
2. The Congress shall have Power to declare the Punishment of Treason, but no Attainder of Treason shall work Corruption of Blood, or Forfeiture except during the Life of the Person attainted.

ARTICLE IV

Section 1

Full Faith and Credit shall be given in each State to the public Acts, Records, and judicial Proceedings of every other State. And the Congress may by general Laws prescribe the Manner in which such Acts, Records and Proceedings shall be proved, and the Effect thereof.

Section 2

1. The Citizens of each State shall be entitled to all Privileges and Immunities of Citizens in the several States.
2. A Person charged in any State with Treason, Felony, or other Crime, who shall flee from Justice, and be found in another State, shall on Demand of the executive Authority of the State from which he fled, be delivered up, to be removed to the State having Jurisdiction of the Crime.
3. No Person held to Service or Labor in one State, under the Laws thereof, escaping into another, shall, in Consequence of any Law or Regulation therein, be discharged from such Service or Labor, but shall be delivered up on Claim of the Party to whom such Service or Labor may be due.

Section 3

1. New States may be admitted by the Congress into this Union; but no new State shall be formed or erected within the Jurisdiction of any other State; nor any State be formed by the Junction of two or more States, or Parts of States, without the Consent of the Legislatures of the States concerned as well as of the Congress.
2. The Congress shall have Power to dispose of and make all needful Rules and Regulations respecting the Territory or other Property belonging to the United States; and nothing in this Constitution shall be so construed as to Prejudice any Claims of the United States, or of any particular State.

Section 4

The United States shall guarantee to every State in this Union a Republican Form of Government, and shall protect each of them against Invasion; and on Application of the Legislature, or of the Executive (when the Legislature cannot be convened) against domestic Violence.

ARTICLE V

The Congress, whenever two thirds of both Houses shall deem it necessary, shall propose Amendments to this Constitution, or, on the Application of the Legislatures of two thirds of the several States, shall call a Convention for proposing Amendments, which, in either Case, shall be valid to all Intents and Purposes, as Part of this Constitution, when ratified by the Legislatures of three fourths of the several States, or by Conventions in three fourths thereof, as the one or the other Mode of Ratification may be proposed by the Congress; Provided that no Amendment which may be made prior to the Year One thousand eight hundred and eight shall in any Manner affect the first and fourth Clauses in the Ninth Section of the first Article; and that no State, without its Consent, shall be deprived of its equal Suffrage in the Senate.

ARTICLE VI

1. All Debts contracted and Engagements entered into, before the Adoption of this Constitution, shall be as valid against the United States under this Constitution, as under the Confederation.
2. This Constitution, and the Laws of the United States which shall be made in Pursuance thereof; and all Treaties made, or which shall be made, under the Authority of the United States, shall be the supreme Law of the Land; and the Judges in every State shall be bound thereby, any Thing in the Constitution or Laws of any State to the Contrary notwithstanding.
3. The Senators and Representatives before mentioned, and the Members of the several State Legislatures, and all executive and judicial Officers, both of the United States and of the several States, shall be bound by Oath or Affirmation, to support this Constitution; but no religious Test shall ever be required as a Qualification to any Office or public Trust under the United States.

ARTICLE VII

The Ratification of the Conventions of nine States, shall be sufficient for the Establishment of this Constitution between the States so ratifying the Same.

DONE in Convention by the Unanimous Consent of the States present the Seventeenth Day of September in the Year of our Lord one thousand seven hundred and eighty-seven and of the Independence of the United States of America the Twelfth IN WITNESS whereof We have hereunto subscribed our Names,

GO. WASHINGTON—President
and deputy from Virginia

[Signed also by the deputies of twelve States.]

New Hampshire
  JOHN LANGDON
  NICHOLAS GILMAN
Massachusetts
  NATHANIEL GORHAM
  RUFUS KING
Connecticut
  WM. SAML. JOHNSON
  ROGER SHERMAN
New York
  ALEXANDER HAMILTON
New Jersey
  WIL. LIVINGSTON
  DAVID BREARLEY
  WM. PATERSON
  JONA. DAYTON
Pennsylvania
  B. FRANKLIN
  THOMAS MIFFLIN
  ROBT MORRIS
  GEO. CLYMER
  THOS. FITZSIMONS
  JARED INGERSOLL
  JAMES WILSON
  GOUV MORRIS
Delaware
  GEO. READ
  GUNNING BEDFORD jun
  JOHN DICKINSON
  RICHARD BASSETT
  JACO. BROOM
Maryland

JAMES MCHENRY
DAN OF ST THOS. JENIFER
DANL CARROLL

Virginia
JOHN BLAIR
JAMES MADISON Jr.

North Carolina
WM BLOUNT
RICHD. DOBBS SPAIGHT
HU WILLIAMSON

South Carolina
J. RUTLEDGE
CHARLES COTESWORTH PINCKNEY
CHARLES PINCKNEY
PIERCE BUTLER

Georgia
WILLIAM FEW
ABR BALDWIN

Attest WILLIAM JACKSON Secretary

AMENDMENTS TO THE CONSTITUTION

Amendment I

Congress shall make no law respecting an establishment of religion, or prohibiting the free exercise thereof; or abridging the freedom of speech, or of the press; or the right of the people peaceably to assemble, and to petition the Government for a redress of grievances.

Amendment II

A well regulated Militia, being necessary to the security of a free State, the right of the people to keep and bear Arms, shall not be infringed.

Amendment III

No Soldier shall, in time of peace be quartered in any house, without the consent of the Owner, nor in time of war, but in a manner to be prescribed by law.

Amendment IV

The right of the people to be secure in their persons, houses, papers, and effects, against unreasonable searches and seizures, shall not be violated, and no Warrants shall issue, but upon probable cause, supported by Oath or affirmation, and particularly describing the place to be searched, and the persons or things to be seized.

Amendment V

No person shall be held to answer for a capital, or otherwise infamous crime, unless on a presentment or indictment of a Grand Jury, except in cases arising in the land or naval forces, or in the Militia, when in actual service in time of War or public danger; nor shall any person be subject for the same offence to be twice put in jeopardy of life or limb; nor shall be compelled in any criminal case to be a witness against himself, nor be deprived of life, liberty, or property, without due process of law; nor shall private property be taken for public use, without just compensation.

Amendment VI

In all criminal prosecutions, the accused shall enjoy the right to a speedy and public trial, by an impartial jury of the State and district wherein the crime shall have been committed, which district shall have been previously ascertained by law, and to be informed of the nature and cause of the accusation; to be confronted with the witnesses against him; to have compulsory process for obtaining witnesses in his favor, and to have the Assistance of Counsel for his defense.

Amendment VII

In Suits at common law, where the value in controversy shall exceed twenty dollars, the right of trial by jury shall be preserved, and no fact tried by a jury, shall be otherwise re-examined in any Court of the United States, then according to the rules of the common law.

Amendment VIII

Excessive bail shall not be required, nor excessive fines imposed, nor cruel and unusual punishments inflicted.

Amendment IX

The enumeration in the Constitution, of certain rights, shall not be construed to deny or disparage others retained by the people.

Amendment X

The powers not delegated to the United States by the Constitution, nor prohibited by it to the States, are reserved to the States respectively, or to the people.

Amendment XI

The Judicial power of the United States shall not be construed to extend to any suit in law or equity, commenced or prosecuted against one of the United States by Citizens of another State, or by Citizens or Subjects of any Foreign State.

Amendment XII

The Electors shall meet in their respective states, and vote by ballot for President and Vice-President, one of whom, at least, shall not be an inhabitant of the same state with themselves; they shall name in their ballots the person voted for as President, and in distinct ballots the person voted for as Vice-President, and they shall make distinct lists of all persons voted for as President, and of all persons voted for as Vice-President, and of the number of votes for each, which lists they shall sign and certify, and transmit sealed to the seat of the government of the United States, directed to the President of the Senate;—The President of the Senate shall, in the presence of the Senate and House of Representatives, open all the certificates and the votes shall then be counted;—The person having the greatest number of votes for President, shall be the President, if such number be a majority of the whole number of Electors appointed; and if no person have such majority, then from the persons having the highest numbers not exceeding three on the list of those voted for as President, the House of Representatives shall choose immediately, by ballot, the President. But in choosing the President, the votes shall be taken by states, the representation from each state having one vote; a quorum for this purpose shall consist of a member or members from two-thirds of the states, and a majority of all the states shall be necessary to a choice. And if the House of Representatives shall not choose a President whenever the right of choice shall devolve upon them, before the fourth day of March next following, then the Vice-President shall act as President, as in the case of the death or other constitutional disability of the President. The person having the greatest number of votes as Vice-President, shall be the Vice-President, if such number be a majority of the whole number of Electors appointed, and if no person have a majority, then from the two highest numbers on the list, the Senate shall choose the Vice-President; a quorum for the purpose shall consist of two thirds of the whole number of Senators, and a majority of the whole number shall be necessary to a choice. But no person constitutionally ineligible to the office of President shall be eligible to that of Vice-President of the United States.

Amendment XIII

Section 1

Neither slavery nor involuntary servitude, except as a punishment for crime whereof the party shall have been duly convicted, shall exist within the United States, or any place subject to their jurisdiction.

Section 2

Congress shall have power to enforce this article by appropriate legislation.

Amendment XIV

Section 1

All persons born or naturalized in the United States, and subject to the jurisdiction thereof, are citizens of the United States and of the State wherein they reside. No State shall make or enforce any law which shall abridge the privileges or immunities of citizens of the United States; nor shall any State deprive any person of life, liberty, or property, without due process of law; nor deny to any person within its jurisdiction the equal protection of the laws.

Section 2

Representatives shall be apportioned among the several States according to their respective numbers, counting the whole number of persons in each State, excluding Indians not taxed. But when the right to vote at any election for the choice of electors for President and Vice President of the United States, Representatives in Congress, the Executive and Judicial officers of a State, or the members of the Legislature thereof, is denied to any of the male inhabitants of such State, being twenty-one years of age, and citizens of the United States, or in any way abridged, except for participation in rebellion, or other crime, the basis of representation therein shall be reduced in the proportion which the number of such male citizens shall bear to the whole number of male citizens twenty-one years of age in such State.

Section 3

No person shall be a Senator or Representative in Congress, or elector of President and Vice President, or hold any office, civil or military, under the United States, or under any State, who, having previously taken an oath, as a member of Congress, or as an officer of the United States, or as a member of any State legislature, or as an executive or judicial officer of any State, to support the Constitution of the United States, shall have engaged in insurrection or rebellion against the same, or given aid or comfort to the enemies thereof. But Congress may by a vote of two-thirds of each House, remove such disability.

Section 4

The validity of the public debt of the United States, authorized by law, including debts incurred for payment of pensions and bounties for services in suppressing insurrection or rebellion, shall not be questioned. But neither the United States nor any State shall assume or pay any debt or obligation incurred in aid of insurrection or rebellion against the United States, or any claim for the loss or emancipation of any slave; but all such debts, obligations and claims shall be held illegal and void.

Section 5

The Congress shall have power to enforce, by appropriate legislation, the provisions of this article.

Amendment XV

Section 1

The right of citizens of the United States to vote shall not be denied or abridged by the United States or by any State on account of race, color, or previous condition of servitude.

Section 2

The Congress shall have power to enforce this article by appropriate legislation.

Amendment XVI

The Congress shall have power to lay and collect taxes on incomes, from whatever source derived, without apportionment among the several States, and without regard to any census or enumeration.

Amendment XVII

The Senate of the United States shall be composed of two Senators from each State, elected by the people thereof, for six years; and each Senator shall have one vote. The electors in each State shall have the qualifications requisite for electors of the most numerous branch of the State legislatures. When vacancies happen in the representation of any State in the Senate, the executive authority of such State shall issue writs of election to fill such vacancies: Provided, That the legislature of any State may empower the executive thereof to make temporary appointments until the people fill the vacancies by election as the legislature may direct. This amendment shall not be so construed as to affect the election or term of any Senator chosen before it becomes valid as part of the Constitution.

Amendment XVIII

Section 1

After one year from the ratification of this article the manufacture, sale, or transportation of intoxicating liquors within, the importation thereof into, or the exportation thereof from the United States and all territory subject to the jurisdiction thereof for beverage purposes is hereby prohibited.

Section 2

The Congress and the several States shall have concurrent power to enforce this article by appropriate legislation.

Section 3

This article shall be inoperative unless it shall have been ratified as an amendment to the Constitution by the legislatures of the several States, as provided in the Constitution, within seven years from the date of the submission hereof to the States by the Congress.

Amendment XIX

The right of citizens of the United States to vote shall not be denied or abridged by the United States or by any State on account of sex. Congress shall have power to enforce this article by appropriate legislation.

Amendment XX

Section 1

The terms of the President and Vice President shall end at noon on the 20th day of January, and the terms of Senators and Representatives at noon on the 3d day of January, of the years in which such terms would have ended if this article had not been ratified; and the terms of their successors shall then begin.

Section 2

The Congress shall assemble at least once in every year, and such meeting shall begin at noon on the 3d day of January, unless they shall by law appoint a different day.

Section 3

If, at the time fixed for the beginning of the term of the President, the President elect shall have died, the Vice President elect shall become President. If a President shall not have been chosen before the time fixed for the beginning of his term, or if the President elect shall have failed to qualify, then the Vice President elect shall act as President until a President shall have qualified; and the Congress may by law provide for the case wherein neither a President elect nor a Vice President elect shall have qualified, declaring who shall then act as President, or the manner in which one who is to act shall be selected, and such person shall act accordingly until a President or Vice President shall have qualified.

Section 4

The Congress may by law provide for the case of the death of any of the persons from whom the House of Representatives may choose a President whenever the right of choice shall have devolved upon them, and for the case of the death of any of the persons from whom the Senate may choose a Vice President whenever the right of choice shall have devolved upon them.

Section 5

Sections 1 and 2 shall take effect on the 15th day of October following the ratification of this article.

Section 6

This article shall be inoperative unless it shall have been ratified as an amendment to the Constitution by the legislatures of three fourths of the several States within seven years from the date of its submission.

Article XXI

Section 1

The eighteenth article of amendment to the Constitution of the United States is hereby repealed.

Section 2

The transportation or importation into any State, Territory, or possession of the United States for delivery or use therein of intoxicating liquors, in violation of the laws thereof, is hereby prohibited.

Section 3

This article shall be inoperative unless it shall have been ratified as an amendment to the Constitution by conventions in the several States, as provided in the Constitution, within seven years from the date of the submission hereof to the States by the Congress.

Amendment XXII

Section 1

No person shall be elected to the office of the President more than twice, and no person who has held the office of President, or acted as President, for more than two years of a term to which some other person was elected President shall be elected to the office of the President more than once. But this Article shall not apply to any person holding the office of President when this Article was proposed by the Congress, and shall not prevent any person who may be holding the office of President, or acting as President, during the term within which this Article becomes operative from holding the office of President or acting as President during the remainder of such term.

Section 2

This article shall be inoperative unless it shall have been ratified as an amendment to the Constitution by the legislatures of three fourths of the several States within seven years from the date of its submission to the States by the Congress.

Amendment XXIII

Section 1

The District constituting the seat of Government of the United States shall appoint in such manner as the Congress may direct: A number of electors of President and Vice President equal to the whole number of Senators and Representatives in Congress to which the District would be entitled if it were a State, but in no event more than the least populous State; they shall be in addition to those appointed by the States, but they shall be considered, for the purposes of the election of President and Vice President, to be electors appointed by a State; and they shall meet in the District and perform such duties as provided by the twelfth article of amendment.

Section 2

The Congress shall have power to enforce this article by appropriate legislation.

Amendment XXIV

Section 1

The right of citizens of the United States to vote in any primary or other election for President or Vice President, for electors for President or Vice President, or for Senator or Representative in Congress, shall not be denied or abridged by the United States or any State by reason of failure to pay any poll tax or other tax.

Section 2

The Congress shall have power to enforce this article by appropriate legislation.

Amendment XXV

Section 1

In case of the removal of the President from office or of his death or resignation, the Vice President shall become President.

Section 2

Whenever there is a vacancy in the office of the Vice President, the President shall nominate a Vice President who shall take office upon confirmation by a majority vote of both Houses of Congress.

Section 3

Whenever the President transmits to the President pro tempore of the Senate and the Speaker of the House of Representatives his written declaration that he is unable to discharge the powers and duties of his office, and until he transmits to them a written declaration to the contrary, such powers and duties shall be discharged by the Vice President as Acting President.

Section 4

Whenever the Vice President and a majority of either the principal officers of the executive departments or of such other body as Congress may by law provide, transmit to the President pro tempore of the Senate and the Speaker of the House of Representatives their written declaration that the President is unable to discharge the powers and duties of his office, the Vice President shall immediately assume the powers and duties of the office as Acting President. Thereafter, when the President transmits to the President pro tempore of the Senate and the Speaker of the House of Representatives his written declaration that no inability exists, he shall resume the powers and duties of his office unless the Vice President and a majority of either the principal officers of the executive department or of such other body as Congress may by law provide, transmit within four days to the President pro tempore of the Senate and the Speaker of the House of Representatives their written declaration that the President is unable to discharge the powers and duties of his office. Thereupon Congress shall decide the issue, assembling within forty-eight hours for that purpose if not in session. If the Congress, within twenty-one days after receipt of the latter written declaration, or, if Congress is not in session, within twenty-one days after Congress is required to assemble, determines by two thirds vote of both Houses that the President is unable to discharge the powers and duties of his office, the Vice President shall continue to discharge the same as Acting President; otherwise, the President shall resume the powers and duties of his office.

Amendment XXVI

Section 1

The right of citizens of the United States, who are eighteen years of age or older, to vote shall not be denied or abridged by the United States or by any State on account of age.

Section 2

The Congress shall have power to enforce this article by appropriate legislation.

Amendment XXVII

No law, varying the compensation for the services of the Senators and Representatives, shall take effect, until an election of Representatives shall have intervened.

Appendix B
Additional Resources

BOOKS

Jack M. Balkin, Living Originalism (2012).
Randy Barnett, Our Republican Constitution: Securing The Liberty & Sovereignty of We the People (2016).
Randy Barnett, Restoring the Lost Constitution: The Presumption of Liberty (2004).
Randy E. Barnett & Evan D. Bernick, The Original Meaning of the Fourteenth Amendment: Its Letter and Spirit (2021).
Randy E. Barnett & Josh Blackman, An Introduction to Constitutional Law: 100 Supreme Court Cases Everyone Should Know (2019).
Josh Blackman, Unraveled: Obamacare, Religious Liberty, and Executive Power (2016).
Derek Bok & William Bowen, The Shape of the River (1998).
Kristine Bowman (ed.), Oxford Handbook of U.S. Education Law 179 (2021).
Jeffrey A Brauch, Flawed Perfection: What it Means to Be Human and Why It Matters for Culture, Politics, and Law (2017).
Corey Brettschneider (ed.), Free Speech (2021).
Stephen Breyer, Active Liberty (2005).
Stephen Breyer, Making Our Democracy Work: A Judge's View (2010).
Stephen Breyer, The Authority of the Court and the Perils of Politics (2021).
Elizabeth Kaufer Busch & William E. Thro, Title IX: The Transformation of Sex Discrimination in Education (2018).
Sheryll Cashin, Place Not Race: A New Vision of Opportunity In America (2014).
Susan G. Clark & Sandra C. Coyner (eds.), Case Studies in Higher Education: The Law and Administrative Decision Making (2016).
Stephen V. Coffin (ed.), Overcoming the Educational Equity Gap (2022).

Stephen V. Coffin (ed.), Higher Education's Looming Collapse: Using New Ways Of Doing Business and Social Justice to Avoid Bankruptcy (2021).
Andrew Doyle, Free Speech and Why It Matters (2022).
Daniel L. Dreisbach, Reading the Bible with the Founding Fathers (2017).
Ronald Dworkin, Law's Empire (1986).
John Hart Ely, Democracy and Distrust: A Theory of Judicial Review (1982).
Matthew W. Finkin & Robert C. Post, For the Common Good: Principles of American Academic Freedom (2009).
Stanley Fish, Versions of Academic Freedom: From Professionalism to Revolution (2014).
Stanley Fish, Save the World on Your Own Time (2008).
Daniel F. Forte & Matthew Spalding (eds.), The Heritage Guide to the Constitution (2nd ed. 2014).
David French, Divided We Fall: America's Secession Threat and How to Restore Our Nation (2020).
Neil Gorsuch, A Republic, If You Can Keep It (2019).
Os Guinness, A Free People's Suicide (2013).
Os Guinness, The Magna Carta of Humanity: Sinai's Revolutionary Faith and the Future of Freedom (2021).
Os Guinness, Last Call for Liberty: How America's Genius for Freedom Has Become Its Greatest Threat (2018).
Mark David Hall, Did America Have a Christian Founding?: Separating Modern Myth from Historical Truth (2019).
Mark David Hall, Roger Sherman and the Creation of the American Republic (2013).
Phillip Hamburger, Separation of Church and State (2003).
Daniel Hannan, Inventing Freedom: How the English-Speaking Peoples Made the Modern World (2013).
Richard Hofstadter & Walter P. Metzger, The Development of Academic Freedom in the United States 386–91 (1955).
A.E. Dick Howard, The Road from Runnymede: Magna Carta and Constitutionalism in America (1968).
John D. Inazu, A Confident Pluralism: Surviving and Thriving Through Deep Difference (2016).
John Inazu & Tim Keller (eds.), Uncommon Ground: Living Faithfully in a World of Difference (2020).
William A. Kaplin, Barbara A. Lee, Neal H. Hutchens, & Jacob A. Rooksby, The Law of Higher Education (6th ed. 2020).
Randall Kennedy, For Discrimination: Race, Affirmative Action, & the Law (2013).
Charles R. Kesler, Crisis of the Two Constitutions: The Rise, Decline, and Recovery of American Greatness (2021).
Peter Lake (ed.), Oxford Handbook of U.S. Higher Education Law (forthcoming 2022).
Peter Augustine Lawler & Richard M. Reinsch, A Constitution in Full: Recovering the Unwritten Foundation of American Liberty (2019).

Martin Loughlin, THE BRITISH CONSTITUTION: A VERY SHORT INTRODUCTION (2013).
Greg Lukianoff, UNLEARNING LIBERTY: CAMPUS CENSORSHIP AND THE END OF AMERICAN DEBATE (2012).
Greg Lukianoff & Jonathon Haidt, THE CODDLING OF THE AMERICAN MIND: HOW GOOD INTENTIONS AND BAD IDEAS ARE SETTING UP A GENERATION FOR FAILURE (2018).
Heather MacDonald, THE DIVERSITY DELUSION: HOW RACE AND GENDER PANDERING CORRUPT THE UNIVERSITY AND UNDERMINE OUR CULTURE (2018).
Pauline Maier, RATIFICATION: THE PEOPLE DEBATE THE CONSTITUTION (2010).
Michael W. McConnell, Robert F. Corchran, Jr., & Angela C. Carmella (eds.), CHRISTIAN PERSPECTIVES ON LEGAL THOUGHT (2001).
Eric Metaxas, IF YOU CAN KEEP IT: THE FORGOTTEN PROMISE OF AMERICAN LIBERTY (2016).
William Lee Miller, THE FIRST LIBERTY: AMERICA'S FOUNDATION IN RELIGIOUS FREEDOM (1986).
Russell K. Nieli, WOUNDS THAT WILL NOT HEAL: AFFIRMATIVE ACTION AND OUR CONTINUING RACIAL DIVIDE (2012).
John T. Noonan, Jr., NARROWING THE NATION'S POWER: THE SUPREME COURT SIDES WITH THE STATES (2002).
Robert M. O'Neil, FREE SPEECH IN THE COLLEGE COMMUNITY (1997).
Robert M. O'Neil, ACADEMIC FREEDOM IN THE WIRED WORLD: POLITICAL EXTREMISM, CORPORATE POWER, AND THE UNIVERSITY (2008).
Robert M. O'Neil, THE FIRST AMENDMENT & CIVIL LIABILITY (2001).
Michael Stokes Paulsen & Luke Paulsen, THE CONSTITUTION: AN INTRODUCTION (2015).
Nathaniel Philbrick, MAYFLOWER: A STORY OF COURAGE, COMMUNITY, AND WAR (2006).
Steven G. Poskanzer, HIGHER EDUCATION LAW: THE FACULTY (2002).
Robert C. Post, DEMOCRACY, EXPERTISE, AND ACADEMIC FREEDOM: A FIRST AMENDMENT JURISPRUDENCE FOR THE MODERN STATE (2012).
Kirsten Powers, THE SILENCING: HOW THE LEFT IS KILLING FREE SPEECH (2015).
Jonathan Rauch, THE CONSTITUTION OF KNOWLEDGE (2021).
Michael A. Rebell, COURTS AND KIDS: PURSUING EDUCATIONAL EQUITY THROUGH THE STATE COURTS (2009).
William Rehnquist, THE SUPREME COURT (2001).
Henry Reichman, UNDERSTANDING ACADEMIC FREEDOM (2021).
Ralph Rossum, ANTONIN SCALIA'S JURISPRUDENCE: TEXT AND TRADITION (2006).
Charles J. Russo (ed.), ENCYCLOPEDIA OF LAW AND HIGHER EDUCATION (2010).
Richard Sander & Stuart Taylor, Jr., MISMATCH: HOW AFFIRMATIVE ACTION HURTS STUDENTS IT'S INTENDED TO HELP AND WHY UNIVERSITIES WON'T ADMIT IT (2012).
Antonin Scalia, THE ESSENTIAL SCALIA: ON THE CONSTITUTION, THE COURTS, AND THE RULE OF LAW (Jeffrey S. Sutton & Edward Whelan, eds., 2020).
Antonin Scalia, ON FAITH: LESSON FROM AN AMERICAN BELIEVER (Christopher J. Scalia & Edward Whelan, eds., 2019).
Antonin Scalia, A MATTER OF INTERPRETATION: FEDERAL COURTS AND THE LAW (Amy Gutmann ed., 1997).
Antonin Scalia, SCALIA'S COURT: A LEGACY OF LANDMARK OPINIONS AND DISSENTS (Kevin A. Ring, ed., 2016).

Antonin Scalia, SCALIA SPEAKS: REFLECTIONS ON LAW, FAITH, AND LIFE WELL LIVED (Christopher J. Scalia & Edward Whelan, eds., 2017).
Antonin Scalia & Bryan A. Garner, MAKING YOUR CASE: THE ART OF PERSUADING JUDGES (2000).
Antonin Scalia & Bryan A. Garner, READING LAW: THE INTERPRETATION OF LEGAL TEXTS (2012).
David Starkey, MAGNA CARTA: THE MEDIEVAL ROOTS OF MODERN POLITICS (2015).
Lee J. Strang, ORIGINALISM'S PROMISE: A NATURAL LAW ACCOUNT OF THE CONSTITUTION (2019).
Alexis de Tocqueville, DEMOCRACY IN AMERICA (1835).
Stephen Tomkins, THE JOURNEY TO THE MAYFLOWER: GOD'S OUTLAWS AND THE INVENTION OF FREEDOM (2020).
John G. Turner, THEY KNEW THEY WERE PILGRIMS: PLYMOUTH COLONY AND THE CONTEST FOR AMERICAN LIBERTY (2020).
Adrian Vermeule, COMMON GOOD CONSTITUTIONALISM (2022).
Keith E. Whittington, SPEAK FREELY: WHY UNIVERSITIES MUST DEFEND FREE SPEECH (2018).
Joanna Williams, ACADEMIC FREEDOM IN AN AGE OF CONFORMITY (2016).
Gordon Wood, THE CREATION OF THE AMERICAN REPUBLIC, 1776–1787 (1998 ed.).
Gordon S. Wood, POWER & LIBERTY: CONSTITUTIONALISM IN THE AMERICAN REVOLUTION (2021).
James Wood, FIRST FREEDOM: RELIGION AND THE BILL OF RIGHTS (1990).
Peter Wood, 1620: A CRITICAL RESPONSE TO THE 1619 PROJECT (2020).
Colin Woodard, AMERICAN NATIONS: A HISTORY OF THE ELEVEN REGIONAL CULTURES OF NORTH AMERICA (2011).
Emily Zackin, LOOKING FOR RIGHTS IN ALL THE WRONG PLACES: WHY STATE CONSTITUTIONS CONTAIN AMERICA'S POSITIVE RIGHTS (2013).

ARTICLES IN SCHOLARLY JOURNALS

Lynn A. Baker, *The Revival of States' Rights: A Progress Report and a Proposal*, 22 HARV. J.L. & PUB. POL. 95 (1998).
Jack M. Balkin, *Framework Originalism and the Living Constitution*, 103 N.W. L. REV. 549 (2009).
Jonathan Banks, *State Constitutional Analyses of Public-School Finance Reform Cases: Myth or Methodology?* 45 VAND. L. REV. 129, 156 (1992).
Will Baude, *Originalism as a Constraint on Judges*, 84 U. CHI. L. REV. 2213 (2017).
Scott R. Bauries, *Individual Academic Freedom: An Ordinary Concern of the First Amendment*, 83 MISS. L. 677 (2014).
Scott R. Bauries, *Is There an Elephant in the Room?: Judicial Review of Educational Adequacy and The Separation of Powers in State Constitutions,* 61 ALA. L. REV. 701, 760-61 (2010).
Scott R. Bauries, *State Constitutions and Individual Rights: Conceptual Convergence in School Finance Litigation*, 18 GEO. MASON L. REV. 301 (2011).

Scott R. Bauries, *The Education Duty*, 47 WAKE FOREST L. REV. 705 (2012).

Scott R. Bauries, *Perversity as Rationality in Teacher Evaluation*, 72 ARK. L. REV. 325 (2019).

Scott R. Bauries, *Neoformalist Constitutional Construction and Public Employee Speech*, 21 U. PA. J. CONST. L. 439 (2018).

Scott R. Bauries, *Professor Williams and the Education Rights in State Constitutional Law*, 72 RUTGERS U. L. REV. 1145 (2020).

Scott R. Bauries & Patrick Schach, *Coloring Outside the Lines: Garcetti v. Ceballos in the Federal Appellate Courts*, 262 ED. LAW REP. 357 (2011).

Josh Blackman, *The Irrepressible Myths of Cooper v. Aaron*, 107 Geo. L.J. 1135 (2019).

Kristi L. Bowman, *A New Strategy for Pursuing Racial and Ethnic Equality in Public Schools*, 1 DUKE F. FOR L. & SOC. CHANGE 47 (2009).

William J. Brennan, *State Constitutions and the Protection of Individual Rights*, 90 HARV. L. REV. 489 (1977).

George D. Brown, *Binding Advisory Opinions: A Federal Court's Perspective on the State School Finance Decisions*, 35 B.C. L. REV. 543 (1994).

J. Peter Byrne, *Neo-Orthodoxy in Academic Freedom*, 88 TEX. L. REV. 143 (2009).

Steven G. Calabresi & Livia G. Fine, *Two Cheers for Professor Balkin's Originalism*, 103 N.W. L. REV. 663 (2009).

Henry L. Chambers, Jr., *Reasonable Certainty and Reasonable Doubt*, 81 MARQ. L. REV. 655 (1998).

Erwin Chemerinsky, *Unanswered Questions: October Term 2003*, 7 GREENBAG 2nd 323 (2004).

David S. Cohen, *Title IX: Beyond Equal Protection*, 28 HARV. J.L. & GENDER 217 (2005).

Todd A. DeMitchell, David T. Herbert, & Loan T. Phan, *The University Curriculum, and the Constitution: Personal Beliefs and Professional Ethics in Graduate School Counseling Programs*, 39 J.C. & U.L. 303 (2013).

Frank H. Easterbrook, *Statutes' Domains*, 50 U. CHI. L. REV. 533 (1983).

Matthew W. Finkin, *Intramural Speech, Academic Freedom, and the First Amendment*, 66 TEX. L. REV. 1323 (1988).

Abner S. Greene, *What Is Constitutional Obligation?*, 93 B.U. L. REV. 1239 (2013).

David L. Gregory & Charles J. Russo, *Proposals to Counter Continuing Resistance to the Implementation of Ex Corde Ecclesiae.*, 74 ST. JOHN'S LAW REVIEW 629 (2000).

Oren R. Griffin, *A View of Campus Safety Law in Higher Education and the Merits of Enterprise Risk Management*, 61 WAYNE L. REV. 379 (2016).

Erica Black Grubb, *Breaking the Language Barrier: The Right to Bilingual Education*, 9 HARV. C.R.-C.L.L. REV. 52, (1974).

Helen Hershkoff, *Positive Rights and State Constitutions: The Limits of Federal Rationality Review*, 112 HARV. L. REV. 1131 (1999).

Paul Horwitz, *Universities as First Amendment Institutions: Some Easy Answers and Hard Questions*, 54 UCLA L. REV. 1497 (2007).

A.E. Dick Howard, *The Renaissance of State Constitutional Law*, 1 EMERGING ISSUES IN STATE CONSTITUTIONAL LAW 1 (1988).

A.E. Dick Howard, *State Courts and Constitutional Rights in the Day of the Burger Court*, 62 VA. L. REV. 873 (1976).

William H. Hurd, *Gone with the Wind? VMI's Loss and the Future of Single-Sex Public Education*, 4 DUKE J. GENDER L. & POL'Y 27 (1997).

Neal H. Hutchens, *Preserving the Independence of Public Higher Education: An Examination of State Constitutional Autonomy Provisions for Public Colleges and Universities*, 35 J.C. & U.L. 271 (2009).

John Inazu, *The Purpose (and Limits) of the University*, 2018 UTAH L. REV. 943 (2018).

Amalia D. Kessler, *Our Inquisitorial Tradition: Equity Procedure, Due Process, and the Search for an Alternative to the Adversarial*, 90 CORNELL L. REV. 1181 (2005).

Peter N. Kirasnow, *Race Discrimination Rationalized Again*, 2015–16 CATO SUP. CT. REV. 59 (2016).

William S. Koski, *Of Fuzzy Standards and Institutional Constraints: A Re-examination of the Jurisprudential History of Educational Finance Reform Litigation*, 43 SANTA CLARA L. REV. 1185, (2003).

William S. Koski & Rob Reich, *When "Adequate" Isn't: The Retreat from Equity in Educational Law and Policy and Why It Matters*, 56 EMORY L.J. 545 (2006).

Douglas Laycock, *Religious Liberty and the Culture Wars*, 2014 U. ILL. L. REV. 839 (2014).

Douglas Laycock, *Theology Scholarships, The Pledge of Allegiance, and Religious Liberty: Avoiding the Extremes*, 118 HARV. L. REV. 155 (2004).

Christopher C. Lund, *Religious Freedom after Gonzales*, 55 S.D. LAW REVIEW 467 (2011).

Michael W. McConnell, *Establishment and Disestablishment at the Founding, Part I: Establishment of Religion*, 44 WM. & MARY L. REV. 2105 (2003).

Michael W. McConnell, *Why Is Religious Liberty the "First Freedom"?*, 21 CARDOZO L. REV. 1243 (2000).

Stephen R. McCullough, *A Vanishing Virginia Constitution?*, 46 U. RICH. L. REV. 347 (2011).

Robert F. McDonnell, *First Principles for Virginia's Fifth Century*, 41 U. RICH. L. REV. 1 (2006).

Molly S. McUsic, *The Future of Brown v. Board of Education: Economic Integration of the Public Schools*, 117 HARV. L. REV. 1334 (2004).

Walter P. Metzger, *Profession and Constitution: Two Definitions of Academic Freedom in America*, 66 TEX. L. REV. 1265 (1988).

Janet Napolitano, *"Only Yes Means Yes": An Essay on University Policies Regarding Sexual Violence and Sexual Assault*, 33 YALE L. & POL'Y REV 387 (2014).

Jim Newberry, *After the Dear Colleague Letter: Developing Enhanced Due Process Protections for Title IX Sexual Assault Cases at Public Institutions*, 44 J.C. & U.L. 78 (2018).

Larry J. Obhof, *School Finance Litigation and the Separation of Powers*, 45 MITCHELL HAMLINE L. REV. 539 (2019).

Michael Stokes Paulsen, *Disaster: The Worst Religious Freedom Case in Fifty Years*, 24 REGENT U. L. REV. 283 (2012).

Michael Stokes Paulsen, *The Most Dangerous Branch: Executive Power to Say What the Law Is*, 83 GEO. L.J. 217 (1994).

David M. Rabban, *Functional Analysis of "Individual" and "Institutional" Academic Freedom Under the First Amendment*, 53 LAW & CONTEMP. PROBS. 227 (1990).

Gershon M. Ratner, *A New Legal Duty for Urban Public Schools: Effective Education in Basic Skills*, 63 TEX. L. REV. 777 (1985).

Diane L. Rosenfeld, *Uncomfortable Conversations: Confronting the Reality of Target Rape on Campus*, 128 HARV. L. REV. F. 359 (2015).

Diane L. Rosenfeld, *Uncomfortable Conversations: Confronting the Reality of Target Rape on Campus*, 128 HARV. L. REV. F. 359 (2015).

Nicholas Quinn Rosenkranz, *The Objects of the Constitution*, 63 STAN. L. REV. 1005 (2011).

James E. Ryan, *Sheff, Segregation, and School Finance Litigation*, 74 N.Y.U. L. REV. 529 (1999).

James E. Ryan, *Standards, Testing, and School Finance Litigation*, 86 TEX. L. REV. 1223 (2008).

Charles J. Russo, *Is Religion the Lost Diversity in Education in an Era of "Militant Secularists?"* 21 UNIVERSITY OF NOTRE DAME AUSTRALIA LAW REVIEW 1 (2020).

Charles J. Russo, *American Legion v. The American Humanist Association and the Bladensburg Cross: Implications for Education*, 46 RELIGION & EDUCATION 482 (2019).

Charles J. Russo, *Trigger Warnings, Safe Spaces, and Free Speech: Lessons from the United States*, 22 INTERNATIONAL JOURNAL OF LAW & EDUCATION 4 (2019).

Charles J. Russo, *The Courts and Education Law: What Role Should Judges Play*, 13 INTERNATIONAL JOURNAL OF EDUCATION LAW AND POLICY 7 (2017).

Charles J. Russo, *Religious Freedom in Education: A Fundamental Human Right*, 42 RELIGION & EDUCATION 17 (2015).

Charles J. Russo, *Fisher v. University of Texas Redux and Race-Conscious Admissions Policies: A Never-Ending Saga?* 18 EDUCATION LAW JOURNAL 111 (2017).

Charles J. Russo, *Fisher v. University of Texas: The Beginning of the End or the End of the Beginning of Race Conscious Admissions Plans in Higher Education in the United States?* 14 EDUCATION LAW JOURNAL 284 (2013).

Charles J. Russo & Paul McGeal, *Religious Freedom in American Catholic Higher Education*, 39 RELIGION & EDUCATION 116 (2012).

Charles J. Russo & Susan J. Scollay, *All Male State-Funded Military Academies: Anachronism or Necessary Anomaly?* 82 EDUCATION LAW REPORTER 1073 (1993).

Charles J. Russo & William E. Thro, *Higher Education Implications of Parents Involved for Community Schools*, 35 JOURNAL OF COLLEGE & UNIVERSITY LAW 239 (2009).

Charles J. Russo & William E. Thro, *The Constitutional Rights of Politically Incorrect Groups: Christian Legal Society v. Walker as an Illustration*, 33 JOURNAL OF COLLEGE & UNIVERSITY LAW 361 (2007).

Paul E. Salamanca, *Snyder v. Phelps: A Hard Case That Did Not Make Bad Law*, 2011 CATO SUP. CT. REV. 57 (2011).

Paul E. Salamanca, *Quo Vadis: The Continuing Metamorphosis of the Establishment Clause Toward Substantive Neutrality*, 41 BRANDEIS L.J. 575 (2003).

Paul E. Salamanca, *The Liberal Polity and Illiberalism in Religious Traditions*, 4 BARRY L. REV. 97 (2003).

Antonin Scalia, *Originalism: The Lesser Evil*, 57 U. CIN. L. REV. 849, 862 (1989).

Dan Schweitzer, *LaPides v. Board of Regents of the University of Georgia System: A Partial Answer to the Sovereign Immunity-Waiver Conundrum*, 17 NAT'L ENVIR. L.J. 3 (Dec. 2002/Jan 2003).

James H. Smylie, *Madison and Witherspoon: Theological Roots of American Political Thought*, 73 AMERICAN PRESBYTERIANS 155 (1995).

Brian A. Snow & William E. Thro, *Still on the Sidelines: Developing the Non-Discrimination Paradigm Under Title IX*, 3 DUKE JOURNAL OF GENDER LAW & POLICY 1 (1996).

Farnaz Farkish Thompson, *Eliminating a Hostile Environment Towards Colleges & Universities: An Examination of the Office for Civil Rights' Unconstitutional Process and Practices*, 28 REGENT U. L. REV. 225 (2016).

William E. Thro, *Who, What, Why, & How: Reimagining State Constitutional Analysis in School Finance Litigation*, 2020 BRIGHAM YOUNG UNIVERSITY EDUCATION & LAW JOURNAL 30 (2021).

William E. Thro, *Follow the Truth Wherever It May Lead: The Supreme Court's Truths and Myths of Academic Freedom*, 45 DAYTON LAW REVIEW 261 (2020).

William E. Thro, *Embracing Constitutionalism: The Court and the Future of Higher Education Law*, 44 DAYTON LAW REVIEW 147 (2019).

William E. Thro, *No Angels in Academe: Ending the Constitutional Deference to Public Higher Education*, 5 BELMONT LAW REVIEW 27 (2018).

William E. Thro, *No Clash of Constitutional Values: Respecting Freedom & Equality in Public University Sexual Assault Cases*, 28 REGENT UNIVERSITY LAW REVIEW 197 (2016).

William E. Thro, *Judicial Humility: The Enduring Legacy of Rose v. Council for Better Education*, 98 KENTUCKY LAW JOURNAL 717 (2010).

William E. Thro, *A New Approach to State Constitutional Analysis in School Finance Litigation*, 14 JOURNAL OF LAW & POLITICS 525 (1998).

William E. Thro, *Judicial Analysis During the Third Wave of School Finance Litigation: The Massachusetts Decision as a Model*, 35 BOSTON COLLEGE LAW REVIEW 597 (1994).

William E. Thro, Note, *To Render Them Safe: The Analysis of State Constitutional Provisions in Public School Finance Reform Litigation*, 75 VIRGINIA LAW REVIEW 1639 (1989).

Timothy M. Tymkovich, *Are State Constitutions Constitutional?* 97 MINN. L. REV. 1802 (2013).

Timothy M. Tymkovich, John Daniel Daily, & Paul Farley, *A Tale of Three Theories: Reason and Prejudice in the Battle for Amendment 2*, 68 U. COLO. L. REV. 287 (1997).

Joshua E. Weishart, *Equal Liberty in Proportion*, 59 WM. & MARY L. REV. 215 (2017).

Joshua E. Weishart, *Aligning Education Rights and Remedies*, 27 KAN. J.L. & PUB. POL'Y 346 (2018).

Robert Williams, *Equality Guarantees in State Constitutional Law*, 63 TEX. L. REV. 1195 (1985).

R. Craig Wood, *Justiciability, Adequacy, Advocacy, and the "American Dream,"* 92 KY. L.J. 739 (2010).

MISCELLANEOUS RESOURCES

American Association of University Professors, DECLARATION OF PRINCIPLES (1915).

American Association of University Professors, STATEMENT OF PRINCIPLES ON ACADEMIC FREEDOM AND TENURE (1940).

ARTICLES OF CONFEDERATION.

Joseph Biden, REMARKS BY PRESIDENT BIDEN CELEBRATING INDEPENDENCE DAY AND INDEPENDENCE FROM COVID 19 (2021).

Frederick Douglass, WHAT TO THE SLAVE IS THE FOURTH OF JULY (1852).

Langston Hughes, LET AMERICA BE AMERICA AGAIN (1935).

Martin Luther King, I Have A Dream (1963).

Martin Luther King, LETTER FROM THE BIRMINGHAM JAIL (1963).

Learned Hand, THE SPIRIT OF LIBERTY (1944).

Abraham Lincoln, GETTYSBURG ADDRESS (1863).

MAYFLOWER COMPACT (1620).

Ronald Reagan, A TIME FOR CHOOSING (1964).

Lawrence Solum, STATEMENT IN SUPPORT OF THE NOMINATION OF THE HONORABLE NEIL M. GORSUCH TO BE AN ASSOCIATE JUSTICE OF THE SUPREME COURT OF THE UNITED STATES (2017).

THE FEDERALIST (Alexander Hamilton, John Jay, James Madison).

University of Chicago, STATEMENT ON FREEDOM OF EXPRESSION (2015).

University of Virginia, STATEMENT OF THE COMMITTEE ON FREE EXPRESSION & FREE INQUIRY (2021).

Frank X. Walker, SEEDTIME IN THE COMMONWEALTH: ON THE OCCASION OF THE UNIVERSITY OF KENTUCKY'S SESQUICENTENNIAL (2015).

About the Authors

William E. Thro is General Counsel of the University of Kentucky, former Solicitor General of Virginia, and a constitutional scholar. Over the course of his career, he has served as chief legal officer for both a public flagship research university and a public liberal arts college, litigated constitutional issues in the Supreme Court of the United States and lower appellate courts, taught courses on the Constitution at both the undergraduate and law school levels, and written extensively on constitutional law in education contexts in both the United States and South Africa.

Mr. Thro is the recipient of Stetson University's Kaplin Award (contribution to higher education law & policy scholarship) and the Education Law Association's McGhehey Award (contributions to education law). He is a Fellow of the National Association of College & University Attorneys (higher education scholarship) and a Distinguished Research & Practice Fellow of the National Education Finance Academy (contributions to education finance). He is the President of the National Education Finance Academy, past President of the Education Law Association, Chair of the General Counsel Advisory Committee of the Association of Public and Land Grant Universities, and a member of the NCAA General Counsel Advisory Board.

As the Chief Legal Officer for the University of Kentucky, he provides initiative-taking strategic advice on critical legal and policy issues confronting a land grant research university with an integrated academic medical center, a high-profile athletics program, and an operating budget of over $5 billion. Before assuming his present position in 2012, he spent eight years as the first in-house counsel at Christopher Newport University, a public liberal arts university. Prior to becoming in-house counsel at Christopher Newport, he represented public institutions as an Assistant Attorney General in both Colorado and Virginia.

As Solicitor General of Virginia for four years, he was responsible for the Virginia State Government's U.S. Supreme Court litigation (except capital cases) as well as lower court appeals involving the constitutionality of statutes or politically sensitive issues. He argued two cases in the U.S. Supreme Court and numerous cases in the lower appellate courts. He co-authored seven U.S. Court merits briefs, eleven U.S. Supreme Court amicus briefs, and more than fifty briefs at the petition stage. Two of those briefs won Best Brief Awards from the National Association of Attorneys General (2004 and 2009).

In addition to co-authoring this book and TITLE IX: THE TRANSFORMATION OF SEX DISCRIMINATION IN EDUCATION (2018), he has published more than sixty articles in law reviews or peer-reviewed journals as well as many monographs, book chapters, and encyclopedia entries. His articles on school finance litigation have been cited by the highest courts of twelve States. He is a former Associate Professor of Constitutional Studies at Christopher Newport University and served as adjunct law faculty for both the University of Kentucky and University of Richmond.

A native of Kentucky, he received his undergraduate degree *summa cum laude* from Hanover College. In addition to receiving the Crowe Citation as the outstanding male in his class, he was the first Hanover student to become a Harry S. Truman Scholar. He earned a graduate degree w*ith honours* from the University of Melbourne while attending as a Rotary Foundation International Ambassadorial Scholar. His law degree is from the University of Virginia where he was a published member of the VIRGINIA LAW REVIEW and research assistant to constitutional law professor A.E. Dick Howard. He began his legal career as a judicial clerk to the late Judge Ronald E. Meredith of the U.S. District Court for the Western District of Kentucky in Louisville.

Mr. Thro writes in his personal capacity and not as General Counsel of the University of Kentucky. This Book does not necessarily reflect the legal positions of the University of Kentucky.

Charles J. Russo is the Joseph Panzer Chair in Education in the University of Dayton School of Education and Health Sciences, Director of its Ph.D. Program, and Research Professor of Law in the University of Dayton School of Law. He is the 1998–1999 President of the Education Law Association, the 2002 recipient of its McGhehey Award (contributions to education law), and 2021 recipient of a Lifetime Achievement Award from the South Africans Education Law Association. Dr. Russo has authored or co-authored more than 325 articles in peer-reviewed journals; authored, co-authored, edited, or co-edited seventy-five books, and has more than 1,200 publications primarily focusing on issues in Education Law. He has spoken extensively on issues in Education Law in the United States and other countries. In addition, he edits two academic journals and serves on more than one dozen editorial boards.

Along with having spoken in thirty-four America States and thirty-one countries outside of the United States on six continents, Dr. Russo has taught summer courses in England, Spain, and Thailand. Internally, He has served as a Visiting Professor at Queensland University of Technology, the University of Newcastle, and Notre Dame University of Australia, Sydney Campus (Australia); the University of Sarajevo (Bosnia and Herzegovina); South East European University (Tetovo, Macedonia); the Potchefstroom and Mafeking Campuses of North West University (Potchefstrom, South Africa); the University of Malaya (Kuala Lumpur, Malaysia); the University of Sao Paulo (Brazil); Yeditepe University (Istanbul, Turkey); Inner Mongolia University for the Nationalities (Tongliago, Inner Mongolia); Ma'anshan Teacher's College (Ma'anshan, China) and Peking University and Capital Normal University (Beijing, China).

Before joining the University of Dayton faculty as Professor and Chair of the Department of Educational Administration in July 1996, Dr. Russo taught at the University of Kentucky from August 1992 to July 1996 and at Fordham University from September 1989 to July 1992. He taught high school for eight and a half years, both prior to and after graduation from law school. He received a Bachelor of Arts degree in Classical Civilization, Juris Doctor, and Doctor of Education degrees in Educational Administration and Supervision from St. John's University. He received a Master of Divinity degree from the Seminary of the Immaculate Conception. He received a Ph.D. *honoris causa* from Potchefstroom University, now the Potchefstroom Campus of Northwest University (South Africa) for his contributions to Education Law.

www.ingramcontent.com/pod-product-compliance
Lightning Source LLC
Chambersburg PA
CBHW032026230426
43671CB00005B/214